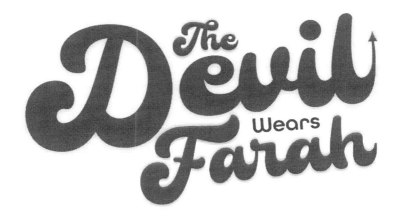

The Devil Wears Farah

By C.J. MacCarthy

umbrella
PUBLISHING

umbrella
PUBLISHING

PUBLISHED BY UMBRELLA PUBLISHING

DUBLIN
IRELAND

First Published 2023

A CIP record for this book is available from the British Library

Cover design and formatting: jessica@viitaladesign.com

Dedication

To the memory of my mother, Lady Fecky (Adelaide), my father, Sean, and especially to my brother, Eoin (Gunga). He died on July 8, 2014, and so, truthfully, did the best laughs.

Contents

Acknowledgements

All my family and friends who gave me the encouragement to keep going when my innate laziness and always feeble capacity to concentrate wanted me to quit and go back to talking about how 'someone', 'someday' should write a book about that time and that place. Siobhan, Adelaide, and Orla were brilliant. Fiona and Mahon were stellar and will know what I wanted to do and why. So will my cousins in Dublin and Cork. Special mention for Eddie W. and Peter C., Peter Mc, Tommy 'Tucker' Greene (RIP), Dee Russell, John Keating, Brian Gray, Mick Clifford and Colin Horgan, Pat O'Toole, Marion O'Brien of Boru, Emma Walsh of TLP, UL's Sarah Moore and, obviously, Liam Hayes, who while being patient and helpful just gets on and ***does***. To all my friends and relations in Limerick and everywhere, several of whom will recognise episodes and incidents from their lives that I have shamelessly 'lifted' and transferred to a more convenient and sublime setting: mine. Most of all, I must acknowledge Eileen and Marcus who are the real reason for doing this; if it makes sense to them now, then it worked and was all worthwhile.

C.J. MacCarthy
April 2023

1

The Salmon Spread of Knowledge

I'VE ALWAYS FELT a little deprived by the fact that I can't remember much from early childhood. Mostly because I'm the kind of person who would have been looking around and making mental notes, specifically, and even at that tender age, of those who hadn't given me my due and would have to be settled with later. That lack of detail is made more irritating because I'm constantly reading accounts and articles by actors and actresses who recall with forensic exactitude episodes from their earliest ages, you know the stuff yourself… 'I remember so vividly the midwife smacking my arse and my cry that seemed to come from the depths of my soul, it was at that moment that I decided that I must go to the Gaiety School of Acting'.

But I can't seem to remember anything. That's not strictly true; in the same way as the Queen must have thought that the world outside her palaces smelled of fresh paint, babies' worlds, at least in those days, smelled of talcum and I dimly-but-distinctly recall the all-pervasive cloying clouds. I also remember being held in a neighbour's arms and being able to watch a bus containing my mother trundling into Limerick because the fields around our house had yet to be built on and so we could see all the way down to the main road, just making out the fields of cabbage on Groody Hill and Park through which the road climbed and wended its way into the small grey city.

And I know I wasn't a noisy baby. My older sister says I was bothered by an eczema or some kind of cradle cap that was treated in the traditional manner with a poultice made with minute quantities of herbs pounded into a lotion and left overnight by ancient holy wells with prayers and even old pre-Christian invocations made over it before being applied to my head and face, it was called *Sudocream*.

In the age of selfie, it's difficult to even comprehend how relatively rare it was to take family photographs. My Dublin mother had albums full of her childhood or teenage picnics in Powerscourt or on the lower slopes of the Sugar Loaf. By contrast, my Cork father considered any kind of *al fresco* food consumption outside of 'tay in the bog' or saving hay as intrinsically foppish and un-Irish and certainly not to be celebrated, much less photographed. He subscribed to the more traditional rule that permitted a photo at baptism, with the next acceptable concession to posterity being the hands pressed together, front-toothless, eyes-to-Heaven, First Communion picture. I can only think of three pictures of me taken before my Communion.

In one, I am a baby on my mother's lap in an armchair, with my two-year-old sister squeezed in behind her and all three of us perched on a corner while the most singularly dangerous looking Jack Russell you ever saw occupies the rest of the seat. The second picture is obviously taken at the same time and there's just myself propped into the corner of the chair with my little scabby scalp resting against the chintz. The third picture is taken when I'm about two and I'm wearing those little trousers that had stirrups around your foot and a tiny dishevelled white vest. I've my hands on my head staring out, distraught, teary, anguished and open, a pedal-car version of 'Streetcar' Marlon. I don't know what's happened, but the emotional explosion looks related to the children's biscuit that I've dropped and which, clearly visible on the grass, must be about to be snapped up by the sinister Jack Russell.

'LEEGA… HEY, LEE-GA!'

There's nothing else specific that occurs. There were the two records I was given as a birthday present by a friend of my mother's, who was ladylike[1] and originally from Meath and was therefore excused the terrible lapse in judgement that had her imagining that *They're Changing the Guard at Buckingham Palace* could ever be a suitable gift for the toddler grandson of republicans who had seen them changing the guard on the landings in Kilmainham. The second record she gave was even more unsuitable; the Horst Wessel song of the grammar schools, *Two Little Boys* by Rolf Harris. This was starting to matter again because by the time I was five 'the North' was sliding into the slow-motion bloodbath that was to last 25 years and the black-and-white footage of intercommunal and state-sponsored rioting we watched every evening on RTÉ on our Bush or Pye sets reflected perfectly the black-and-white positions that we unhesitatingly took: our hereditary Orange enemies who had been 'Christopher Robbin' their way around our country for centuries were at it again.

Forget about room on the horse for two. There wasn't enough room on the whole island for us and those fuckers.

I do recall the first day at school as a hurricane of tantrums, tears and snot; I cried so much that I was allowed sit in beside my sister who was in First Class. We moved through 'Juniors' and into 'Seniors', began plasticine modelling with something called 'Mawla' and started on *Dick and Dora* basic readers. There were Dr Seuss primers as well, *Cat In The Hat* and *Green Eggs And Ham*, but they couldn't work for

[1] She herself wore a mantilla to Mass and we understood that her male relations in Oldcastle wore soft hats but were not horse trainers and were, therefore, obviously 'big farmers'.

the same reason that the Grateful Dead wouldn't be able to jam with Brendan Bowyer and The Royal. I was reading quickly, a facility that was more than counterbalanced by an inability with 'Sums' that bordered on a category of special needs – as if that concept even existed then. We all wore wellingtons through the long winters and wet early springs and then, at the first sign of hardening ground, made a herd migration over to Clarks' sandals or 'tackies' – primitive plimsolls. Obviously, there's a danger of my own view being skewed, but there did seem to be a lot of kids with cross-eyes or corrective patches, which must have been caused by the strain of trying to work out which of the stick-on characters in our *Buntus Cainte* was addressing who and giving what to which as they all – Mhamai, Dhadai agus na páistí – floated around facing different ways in zero gravity on the black felt board.

There was a nature table on which were kept a few empty nests, jars of tadpoles and preserved stools from various specimens of small wildlife, and snaily fossils on which we traced the spiral indentations with biro and tongue-poked concentration.

There were two classes to each room, with the teacher switching from one to the other every five minutes like a pre-set garden sprinkler. When it all became too much – as it must regularly have done with 45-odd infants – the teacher would say 'Téigh a chodladh' (Go to sleep) and we all closed our eyes and bent forward to rest on the desks while she recomposed herself. In a narcoleptic fug of wet wool, erratic storage heaters, the sound of soft rain and the smell of crayon gratings, pretending to go asleep naturally became the whole room – including múinteoir herself – falling into 15 or 20 minutes of snug unconsciousness and a cranky awakening with refocus effected through a vigorously conducted ensemble tin-whistling of *Michael, Row The Boat Ashore*.

We did English, Irish, Sums and Catechism, as well as occasional excursions into Geography, Nature and a strange minotaur subject that was half-History and half-Bullshit of the Fianna, Tuatha Dé Danann,

Fionn MacCool and other origin legends that were run seamlessly into Brian Boru and real history. We listened spellbound to the story of how the young Fionn had burned his thumb frying up the salmon of knowledge his poet-teacher had finally caught after decades of trying. When Fionn sucked his thumb to salve the burn, the learning of the ages became his via the magic hazelnuts the salmon had consumed as they fell into his pool in the Boyne.

Something of that magic still lingered into the salmon spread fish paste sandwiches I was given for sos lóin (lunch). Uneaten for weeks, then months, they changed themselves into ravenous mould that ate through the sliced pan wrapper and up the covers of my copybooks till finally making the whole bottom of my school bag disappear one day as we were pouring out the gate to go home. Mortified, I ran all the way home through the forest without breaking a twig.

Somewhere in there, I've a vague recollection of getting the measles or mumps and Seani peering around the door into the darkened room and speaking to me in an unnaturally tender voice. But that's the only time I can remember an air of concern in the house around health; there was a drawer in the press that my mother grandly referred to as 'The Medicine Drawer' that contained three or four different laxatives, Syrup of Figs, Andrews Liver Salts and Milk of Magnesia, and if our complexions deviated from the tribal 'Mick Magnolia' into either 'flushed' or 'peeky', an industrial quantity of one or all was administered with the results being carefully monitored and timed.

I swear to Jesus that I don't think I ever took a tablet and I vividly recall the whole family's bemusement when we were asked on some form or other to nominate the family doctor; we knew doctors – knew what they were and what they did – but we didn't go to them. We might as well have been asked to name the family taxidermist or genealogist. Although a genealogist might have been useful.

The Sunbeam range and several other essential tools of the average family start-up package had been furnished by a legacy left by a granduncle of Seani's who had prospered as a bootlegger before moving into private security consultancy to the Ford Motor Company in Detroit where he specialised in solving union disputes. The ability to distil spirits he had learned in The Gearagh near his Inchigeelagh home and the ability to open heads of stroppy striking workers and their union reps, he seemed to have innately. He had died intestate in some Shady Acres retirement home for shady characters and a firm of American attorneys contacted a firm of South Mall solicitors who were tasked with identifying his Cork relations, all of whom got a share, dependent on their remove from 'Dapper Dan'. Seani's came to something like £1,200 which was a very considerable sum of money in the early 60s.

The provenance of the money that had bought the range and other indispensables for the newly-weds was obviously disreputable, but still, on the cold Christmas nights when we sat together watching RTÉ's main feature, *Some Like It Hot,* we could luxuriate in the heat thrown out by the solid Sunbeam and silently acknowledge Sean's mysterious relation who could have been a model for any of the goons in the 'fillum'. One Christmas I waited till the very last scene of the picture to ask him what he knew about his beneficiary Dan?

'What was he like, Da? What did they say about him? Was he dangerous?' I asked just before Jack Lemmon tears off his wig and confesses to being a man.

Seani said nothing, kept looking at the screen and didn't change expression. Then Joe Brown turned to Jack Lemon and said, 'Well, nobody's perfect'.

He swivelled around to me, raised his arm to point at the television and gave a massive theatrical nod. Nobody was perfect. Osgood had said it as good as anyone could.

My father, Seani, was a complex man and very particular; by Irish standards he hardly swore or cursed and thought that those who did habitually betrayed a lack of intelligence in their inability to express themselves adequately without recourse to 'foul' language. I think I only heard him once take 'God's name in vain'; my mother was in hospital having my youngest sister and Seani was at home minding the other four of us ranging downwards from nine to seven to five and three. Obviously, the thing to do was to take us all to see a James Bond movie and that's how we all ended up sitting with our legs dangling from the seats in the Carlton looking at *Diamonds Are Forever* and noisily licking the orange ice pops that they only served in cinemas and which seemed unaccountably nicer than the ice pops in shops.

'Hi, I'm Plenty,' says Lana Wood.

'But, of course you are!' says James.

'Plenty O'Toole,' continued Lana.

'Named after your father perhaps?' purrs James.

Very distinctly from a couple of seats up, where I knew Seani was from the light of his cigarette, I heard the consternation in his familiar soft Cork lilt: 'Jesus Christ!!'

There was no need for mammy to know that we'd been to the fillums at all, he explained on the way home and sure enough when she returned a few days later with the baby, heavy pleated curtains were drawn over the episode every bit as impressively and signally as they had swished across the Carlton's screen at the end of the movie.

He worked like a dog: he was up and gone before us, six mornings of the week and wasn't back till after we were in bed. We only saw him for any length of time on Sunday or if we were allowed up late, on Saturday night for the Eurovision or some national occasion like that. He had a small wholesale business that involved buying fruit and vegetables from Clancys or Mulrooneys and then driving it out to sell to the small groceries in West Limerick and East Clare where the women could walk down to local small shops for the standard, wholly unprocessed, and bought-that-day dinner.

I couldn't sleep till he was home and developed freakishly acute hearing that enabled me to reach through the pitch-black atmospherics and the rain on the window to pick out his Comer or Bedford truck laboriously climbing up the hill home a full five minutes before a lengthy grinding of gears confirmed that he was reversing down the passage ('avenue' to my mother) that led to the house. If it was cold, and it could be for the six or eight weeks just before Christmas and through to February, then some of the fruit had to be brought in for fear of frosting.

Coming through the door, blue with the cold and holding his frozen hands in front of him like talons where they'd been gripping the steering wheel, he'd shout the household's equivalent of 'All Hands on Deck'.

'BRING IN THE BANANAS!'

At which the eldest three children got out of bed, pulled on wellingtons and anoraks and joined their mother rummaging around in the back of the pitch-dark truck for any 'fancies' like grapes, plums and, specifically, the expensive and high margin Chiquita bananas, which had to be handed down and carried into the house and stacked in a way that would enable him to reload the whole lot quickly the next morning on his own.

While we worked away in the well-honed team we were, he watched from his position backed into the ill-gotten Sunbeam, just visible through the clothes and nappies hung over it to dry overnight, eating his midnight dinner of fried potatoes and little chops, gnawing and thawing slowly and already working through the next day's list: who'd to get what, when and what he'd charge.

I don't think money was the kind of issue it is where there isn't any. He always seemed to have a roll of notes that was produced, opened and nipped in and out of in a movement that was so fast you doubted whether it had happened. Lodgements were made by my mother on Thursdays just before the bank closed to the public in the early afternoon, and if he lodged cheques made out to him or from a third party that subsequently 'bounced' and were sent back to him, they were propped against the butter dish on the kitchen table where he regarded them with a coal-black stare while he leaned against, and drew inspiration from, the kitchen range paid for in stoved-in heads.

He loved all sports but was infatuated with gaelic football and the very mixed fortunes of his native Cork's football teams. When they were eliminated – usually by Kerry – his allegiance was transferred wholeheartedly to that county, where he had lived prior to getting married and where he had won a county senior championship with Kerins O'Rahillys. He understood Kerry as God's last experiment before he achieved Paddy perfection in Cork. He thought golf was a great sport because Lee Trevino, Tony Jacklin or Gary Player had to apply talent; they had to work at the gift they had been given. Talent wasn't enough; the concentration and focus gave you the confidence to trust the talent. Barry John and Gareth Edwards of the sublime Welsh rugby team were not just divinely talented, they had applied themselves in a way that allowed their talent its fullest expression. He was besotted, too, by horse racing and would stand approvingly, jingling the change in his pocket, when we ran past him bent forward and slapping our arses calling out that we were Pat Taaffe on Arkle going away from Mill Run. The smile straightened and the jingling slowed a little if we were Ned Campion on Rockbarton, slowing and marking time before bursting forward with a snort to clear the ironing board and clinch the Agha Khan. Show jumping was suspect: too many bowler hats and Cosgraves at the RDS.

Way too close to the unspeakable chasing the uneatable and way too far from our Sunday afternoon point-to-points where the untweedy watched the unspeedy.

But that was the only sport in which his political antipathies were allowed purchase. In every other outdoor pursuit, he was ecumenical to an exemplary degree. He thought Bob Hiller and David Duckham were adornments to rugby and he understood and appreciated cricket.

Whatever you might think about the English, he would observe, there was no denying their genius for coming up with great games and then arriving at the minutely observed protocols and etiquette that made them great sports. The apogee of this, he felt and told me often, was lawn bowling. The whole cucumber sandwich atmosphere of the game and the gentle 'crumpet's ready' enthusiasm of the players, as they followed their immaculately judged bowls down the rink, was contrasted with the faction fight air of the 'bowels' played on the roads around his native Macroom, where lads took a hundred yards of a run up before elaborately hopping into the air at an agreed mark and wind-milling small cannonballs underarm, off down the road at a velocity that kicked up sparks and meant that the spectators lining the route ahead of the player had skin in the game in the most literal sense conceivable.

The British game was better. It just was.

'You've to give it to them', he'd concede, 'nobody ever had their nose whipped *clane* off lawn bowling.'

The lost love that could not be mentioned was Manchester United. Yes, they were the 'Irish' team. But their treatment of Frank O'Farrell was an insult of Cromwellian vindictiveness. It was not possible to either forgive or forget because Frank was more than Irish; he was Cork, and had been sacrificed in a desperate and useless attempt to mollify the Vodka and Orangeman, George Best. No reconciliation was possible.

HE DIDN'T TAKE holidays and didn't understand them in the normal sense of the word. He would take a day off to go to the Listowel Races, and when he was a garsún and kicking up his heels, he had spent the nights of the weekends in Ballybunion. But only the nights, he'd work during the day. The thought, the *idea*, of a grown man lounging around on a sunbed for a week was incomprehensible to him, but fascinating. He looked at the television ads for JWT holidays in Spain the same wistful way that the people who took JWT holidays in Spain watched advertisements for expensive brands of cigarettes in which beautiful couples floated over the Alps in hot air balloons to a Bossa Nova soundtrack, laughing and smoking and drinking while waving to their friends skiing below.

Our holidays were to my grandmother and our cousins in Dublin, and it was the only time in the year that my mother saw her brother and sister besides the hurried visit on December 8 when we went up for the day shopping. Very understandably, she wanted to convey her pride in her husband and his ability to support his family, and I can recall her burning embarrassment when one year our Wolsey car wouldn't start and, undaunted, Seani manhandled and heaved a full-sized velvet rollback couch into the back of his yellow Comer walkthrough van. He wedged it around with bags of potatoes, put the five children into it under a blanket and then Jaspar Conran'd up a little armchair from boxes of tomatoes for her, before setting off on the four-hour drive to Clonskeagh.

From Naas on, she explained repeatedly, through tears, that when we got to Aunty Madge's we were on no account to get out together and through the rear double doors 'like tinkers'. Instead, we were to climb over and leave through the driver's door individually at five-minute intervals, in specific order, with herself going first. The van was still slowing to a stop when she was out the driver's sliding door, bent double with her high heels clickety-clicking as she scurried across the path and through their gate.

Seani had tea and a pee, and then turned around to drive the four hours back. The next day and to reassure my mother that we were, indeed, not considered tinkers or an *Opportunity Knocks* cover version of the *Beverley Hillbillies*, my aunt picked the most obviously upwardly mobile and exotic day trip then available in Ireland.

Being told we were going to Butlins was the equivalent of being told that we were going to be stepping into another, brighter, lighter dimension of existence where every aspect of being was arranged for the enjoyment of children. The ecstatic giddiness that the announcement brought was so disruptive, and the logistics of getting 10 children and three adults into two cars so convoluted, that it was mid-afternoon when we got to the gates of paradise and the man in the Butlins coat told us that it was too late to go in and we'd have to come back another day.

I burst into tears and told him in front of everyone that he was a 'rotten bastard'… and to make up for that, and in compliance with the national ordinance that held that the only thing to do with a disappointment was to 'offer it up', the little convoy turned around and went to Saint Peter's in Drogheda to look at Blessed (he's been promoted since) Oliver Plunkett's head and say a quick Decade.

That jobsworth on the gate has long gone to his eternal reward (Hell, obviously, which Jimmy Saville has sent back word seems to have been very closely modelled on Butlins Pwllheli in Wales). But sometimes I wish I'd the opportunity to thank him because in breaking my spirit that day he taught me an invaluable lesson and one that would fortify me against all the vicissitudes that fate could dispense. Nothing at all that has happened since can, or could, compare to the sense of betrayal and incandescent fury I felt when having expected to be at least in the presence of water slides, candy floss, a real puppet show staged in a small stripey tent – things that we'd only seen in pictures or on television – I found myself instead looking at a shrunken head that closely resembled a highly polished coconut and being told that, 'Shure, wasn't this every bit as good?'

This was the moment when, being asked to flip over a similarly nut-flavoured fishy offering, I burned my thumb and sucked it. This was my salmon spread of knowledge. If, in that instant, not all the world's learning became mine, then certainly enough came my way to be going on with. Nor could it have been a coincidence that the change, the epiphany, had occurred on the banks of the Boyne, the same river where the empty vessel that was Fionn was filled to brimming.

And the very first piece of knowledge that came my way and which (fair play to me) I've held on to through thick and thin since was the ability to recognise and denounce as 'shite' that which was, indisputably, 'shite'. The second piece of knowledge was the supreme importance of being able to distinguish between the incidentals of a fiasco – the contingent shite – and the essence of the fiasco: the shite-in-itself.

Being asked to pray to an object that looked as if it had fallen through the supporting stilts of a head-hunter's hut in Papua New Guinea was obnoxious and shite – but it was contingent shite. The sense of disappointment and deception I felt was conditional on the anticipation of the pleasure I expected to feel being able to touch and go on a real waterslide or eat candy floss.

The essence of the fiasco, the essence of my sense of betrayal and incandescent fury, was my own expectation, my own anticipation. Disappointment was contingent shite, anticipation was shite-in-itself. The latter was the necessary precondition to the former.

I'm not saying for a minute that I became a 10-year-old miserabilist or some boring pre-pubescent Schopenhauer. But I do recall turning the whole episode over in my mind in the days afterwards and working backwards to the conclusion that it is a mistake to get your hopes up while there is still time for something, anything, to go wrong.

This cautionary principle is commonly known as 'Murphy's Law' and it is surely significant that it is named after the most Irish surname of all.

Other peoples and cultures heard 'Dare to Dream' as an exhortation, as encouragement. We seem to have heard it as either a sneering question or as a threat. Whether that was something as massive as peace and prosperity, or something as minimal as actually getting into Stalag Mosney to see a fucking puppet show. It took a very long time to get to a place where we didn't hear, speak or read those words, 'Dare to Dream', pick-up on the disapproval implicit, and immediately respond mentally with '*No, you're alright, I'm fine as I am, thanks*'.

But we did get there. We got out of our own way and gradually got that sense of remove and perspective necessary to see that we're no different to the others; no better but certainly no worse. And that if the others are permitted to aspire and dream about achievement and fulfilment, then so could we.

The easy thing to do is to attribute the positive change to the abandonment of Catholicism, but that's a mistake. The Catholicism was contingent in the same way that being asked to venerate Oliver Plunkett's head was contingent on being turned away by that bollocks on the gates of Butlins. The essence of the problem, the shite-in-itself, was in us. It's still in there. And the more we shout that it's gone, the less convinced we become.

2

Lord Muck and Lady Feck-Mucky

I SUPPOSE THE very first thing about their mother that normal children will remember is her face or breast or smell. The very first thing I remember about my mother is her right foot, her right ankle to be precise. I was sitting underneath the table and putting fat little hands around her nyloned ankle to feel it flex, just before she pressed down on the pedal of her Singer sewing machine and an urgent electric rattle announced that another seam had been closed. I'm sure I didn't connect anyone particular with the ankle; there's no face attached to this memory.

There's just a nyloned ankle that seems to exist in splendid isolation but is, in fact, already being evaluated in terms of cause-effect. As soon as I was conscious of being conscious, I was determined to stay that way. The only thing I gripped harder than her ankle was a fanatical determination not to go to bed. And I know that it's irritating and silly to hear people pretend that they reached these kinds of conclusions and made these kinds of deductions long before the professors say it's possible or likely. But I'd swear on my heart right now that the very first conscious calculation I made was that after a certain unspecified hour, but one which it was possible to intuit, I had to stop holding the ankle and instead hold my whisht.

If you're not Irish, don't be alarmed there: 'Hold your whisht' is not a euphemism, it just means shutting the fuck up and being silent.

Be still and silent, and wait. The ankle flexed, the whiny electric whirr and then another fold of material fell off the edges of the table to screen off the space underneath, turning it gradually into a little tent within which this mad toddler sat. If I shut up, then 'they' might forget I was there at all. The other voices might drift off, till there was just the sound of the television and the sewing machine breaking the secret silence between adoring me and the most fixated upon ankle since Achilles.

But 'they' always remembered, and my little tent would be invaded by two arms reaching to lift me out and off up to bed. She told me later that she deliberately didn't look in and do the whole singsong 'I can seeee youuuu' baby game, because I wouldn't join in or gurgle any kind of 'Go on so, you got me. Shure... 'twas worth a try'.

She said my default toddler expression was a vaguely unsettling glare, that was initially attributed to a chronic individual case of the national malady: 'trapped wind'. Later, and with a little alarm, she was forced to conclude that the only thing that was trapped in there was, firstly, a genetic predisposition to concealment and, secondly, the ability to throw an explosive hissy-fit if challenged on the first. My older sister, Siobhan, was a perfect and perky baby who had looked over the edge of her crocheted blanket like a kitten playfully peeking over a ball of darn. Cathal, she would say, looked out of the pram like a weasel looking out of a bush.

It's maybe a year later, and I'm still underneath a table with the same ankle. But this time the ankle is fitted into some high heeled patent shoes. And the table isn't an ordinary table; it's one of those chest-high ones with a wide sloping top designed to allow Dickensian ledgers and broadsheet brochures to be rested on and opened by a standing reader. These tables were high enough for children to actually stand-up straight underneath without crouching. That's what I'm doing.

That's what I always seem to be doing. The question is what is she doing in this fabric shop again? And which one is this? Cassidy's or Cannock's or the one down in Sarsfield Street? She's leaning against the table flicking through these dinner tray-sized pattern books and calling out some kind of code to the lady assistants who are all up on sliding ladders to fetch down bolts of cloth from their floor-to-ceiling shelves.

Then they all go over to long polished high counters with inlaid imperial measurements running lengthwise across the top and measuring tapes strewn all over, and huddle around it murmuring till a decisive 'snip' of a heavy fabric scissors announces agreement.

Pleats Jesus! Can they not see how bored I am?

Not just bored, but through boredom and out the other side into irritation and then through that into anger and then through that into self-pity, before finally achieving that Zen-like state of sublime detachment, where you are at one with the chiffon. All you can remember is the boredom and the hours – fucking days, if it was added up – that you spent in those fabric shops and listening to that twaddle about tulle. And for what? Nothing of it mattered or was in any way useful.

Till years and years and years later, you were listening to a woman trying to describe to the company the colour of some beautiful dress she'd seen, or the shade she was thinking about painting the spare bedroom. It wasn't turquoise, she explained. But it wasn't aqua marine, either.

'It was more of a ...more of a.... kind of a...' she struggled on, uncertainly.

That's when, with a little start, you heard yourself piping up, 'Is there not a cyan blue between those two?' And you noticed that while some of the lads laughed and raised a questioning eyebrow, an oddly different light came up in the eyes of the listening women. They looked at you differently straightaway. Warmer. More relaxed. More open. More receptive. You knew what they were thinking: a man who can distinguish between turquoise and aqua marine probably puts the toilet seat down and doesn't vomit with fright if a woman tells him that she'd like to talk about her feelings. They turn to look at you while your face goes from mushroom white to a middle coral with just a flash of fuchsia.

That's all I've got to show for those first years of life when you have to go around with your mother. When you're, literally, at her feet.

I'll be honest: the ability to identify a midnight blue has occasionally paid off and gotten me a blue midnight. But I don't think it was worth it: every other Irishman my age hears *40 Shades of Green* and thinks of Johnny Cash and that lump-in-the-throat view out the cabin window as the plane bringing you back after years abroad banks and you get a first glimpse of our beloved verdant homeland... Paddy's patchwork quilt.

Not me. I think of the endless hours sitting underneath those high tables in Cassidy's Fabrics, with my little bored head resting on my folded arms, while the ladies up the ladders shouted down whether Mrs meant emerald, British racing, shamrock, bottle, fern or forest.

And now I had a name: the ankle and all the rest of it belonged to Adelaide. The woman who beamed down on me and who was the fulcrum around which everything turned was called 'Adelaide' by all the other women who called into our house and were themselves all called Mary or Margaret or Joan or Irene.

Most nights, Margaret Russell walked up to our house in the late darkness for a last cup of coffee, which I was detailed to make. I went next door to the kitchen where I'd pull a chair over to the cooker and standing on it would pour milk into a little pot that was placed over the heat and at which I stared till the erupting bubbles announced it was just about to boil over.

Then holding the handle of the pot in my two hands and balancing carefully on the chair, I'd pour the boiling milk into their two cups and over their coffee granules before climbing down to add their coffee-mate and respective portions of sugar, stir and serve. Years later and genuinely curious, I asked her was she not a little worried about letting a seven-year-old stand on bockety chairs boiling milk for her coffee while she and her pal laughed it up. Was she not worried about my chances of falling and being badly scalded? Not one bit, she said.

I told her that I'd a good mind to report her to social services who – even at this historic remove – would surely want to talk to her about this level of criminal negligence. She said I should go right ahead. That she kept all my school copybooks and reports, and that she'd lodge those as a rebuttal. She was confident that anyone who read those would award her a medal.

The wobbliest thing in that house, she maintained, was her sanity from having to deal with 'feckology' on a daily basis and usually from me.

When the last Mary or Margaret or Joan had gone home, and before I had to run into bed at the faint sound of Seani finishing his long working day and clunking into gear to reverse his truck down the passage to our house, we would sit up, just the two of us. She might have both her sewing and knitting machines on the go, hooking wool around dozens of individual needles that extended to exactly different lengths from the plank-shaped Brother machine that was stowed underneath the couch, calibrating and adjusting the settings of all the dials and settings of these domestic Enigma-machines by consultation with the codes contained in the pattern-books that only she could decipher. I wouldn't be talking anyway, and her mouth was full of pins and needles, so the only person talking in the room was Ironside or Mannix or Big John in *High Chapparal*. She'd look over at me and gasp in exaggerated reaction to some twist in the plot or drama. Except for *The Onedin Line*; she'd stop work completely and perch on the edge of her seat to watch the wind ruffle James Onedin's hair while he stood on the heaving deck of 'The Charlotte Rhodes' and ordered the hoisting of canvas towards a faraway horizon or stared hungrily towards his Liverpudlian home port where the crinoline was pulled up in front of the main mast even faster.

Even with just me there, she'd sit slightly sideways at the front of her chair with her legs crossed at the shins or ankles. She never sprawled or even sat back into a chair; that was ungainly and common.

She didn't make a song and dance about it, but she believed that it was important for women to avoid looking or acting in a way that was 'common'. That meant that she never ate or smoked on the street and that on anything approaching a semi-formal occasion – Mass or a hospital visit or an auction of house contents – she wore gloves. The idea of leaving her house not properly dressed or coiffed in a non-emergency context was practically incomprehensible. She would shake her head just remembering the girls from the North of England who holidayed in Bray and came into town for the day with layers of curlers visible under their head scarfs, setting their hair for the night's dancing in the Arcadia.

Her family had no money, but she had travelled by the 11 bus from her Clonskeagh home – 'built by Crampton's' she would proudly note – into the Loreto on the Green. When that school's choir came on Radio Eireann singing *Is Mise an Tiarna*, which seemed to be roughly every 30 minutes throughout the broadcasting day, she'd trill along in perfect time and mouth-shape as if being conducted by some invisible nun. She considered bad language or cursing to be disgusting and, in a woman, disqualifying. It was impermissible to acknowledge a woman who used language like that; it was beyond 'common', it was in the category below that: 'fishwife'.

The parameters and protocols around what constituted 'common' were opaque and Mitfordesque: if you had to ask why a particular type of face or a way of walking or a tone of voice was 'common' then, in all likelihood, you were 'common' yourself. It was a matter of attitude and innate taste and not a question of money or address. She maintained that reducing the definition of what was or was not 'common' to money or address was itself 'common'. If you asked her to define the opposite of 'common', she would reel off names like Cyd Charisse, Hedy Lemarr, Jean Simmons and Gene Tierney as if they were suburban stations on the way to Grand Central, emphatically announced as… 'Audrey Hepburn'. And, as I've got older, I've started to see how just saying 'Audrey Hepburn' does work as some crazy verbal charm against the possibility of acting – or even thinking – in a way that's 'common'.

Try it yourself if you don't believe me.

Try and imagine Audrey Hepburn and George Peppard crouched over a bonfire made of broken pallets, pissed as parrots on fortified wine, duetting on *Moon River* in a remake entitled *Buckfast at Tiffany's*.

You can try all you want, my Huckleberry friend. But her face won't go in there. George Peppard? Yes. He seems happy enough swigging away and slurring along; he mightn't even be acting.

But her? No. You could be there the rest of your life, but if Audrey's elfin face is in it, then that mental reel won't roll.

The only bad language my mother did allow herself was the multi-purpose 'feck'; so tricky little tasks that involved more effort than they were worth were 'fecky jobs'; while uncertainty or dithering was dismissed as 'fecking and foostering'. Perceived insubordination was given a scientific twist in her frequent announcements that she was, 'sick and tired of putting up with feckology' and if we turned our little noses up at whatever she had cooked, she'd announce grandly, in the voice of the Lord Chamberlain, that 'Lord Muck and Lady Feck-Mucky' would be sitting right where they are now till every bite of that dinner was eaten.

Notwithstanding her permanent sunny disposition and self-censorship on anything that appeared 'common', she had a fantastic touch-paper temper that probably came with having five children under 10 at two-year intervals. Several times daily the frustration around some repeatedly disobeyed order or request would suddenly compress into a little explosion and then a mad footrace between her and the object of her ire to the toilet, the only room in the house with a working lock. If she won, the loser got a smart smack and an urgent clenched-teeth injunction on the exact thinness of the ice they were on. If she lost and you managed to dive through the door, contorting yourself mid-air to turn the key behind you, then five minutes later, you could re-emerge whistling, completely safe in the knowledge that her temper was like one of those squalls disturbing James' ginger locks in *The Onedin Line*... it blew itself out as quickly as it came on.

Herself and himself were completely different in that respect: he'd say nothing but remember everything, she'd blow up but blow over and forget it inside of three minutes. You wouldn't have put them together. I wouldn't and I'm the product of the fact that they did come together. Though he was very sociable and interested in people, he was more reserved and watching. When he met you, he read you and looked and listened for all the clues that told him who you were and what you were like.

From the moment she met you, she was looking for a reason to laugh with you. He was more guarded, and understood and admired those with the ability to disguise what they felt. She thought that life was too short for that kind of caginess; show people what you are and let them decide. She was completely open and deliberately easy to read, was effortlessly funny and thoughtful and inclusive in the unshowy, old-fashioned sense of the word.

They had met in Ballybunion and her being from Dublin and him from Cork, had ended up splitting the difference by settling in Limerick where he worked. They were a good-looking couple and were romantic in the sense that their lives were pooled: there was nothing about either of them that was held back or reserved from the other.

But I can't remember them displaying physical affection or holding hands and the only time I ever heard the pair of them doing something together and laughing with ecstatic abandon was playing swing-ball. At her Loreto School, they had marched from classroom to classroom to the mass singing of *O'Donnell Abu*, but beyond that vague Republicanism of her generation, she wasn't particularly bothered or political. She hadn't his raptor-eye for any manifestation of West Britishness and was blissfully carefree about the religions of her neighbours and friends. She loved going up the mountains behind Sandyford or Rathfarnham to motor bike trials – an activity that would have beeped an 'Orange Intruder' on Seani's Green radar screen – and after watching Victor or Stan on their BSAs or Nortons or Matchless machines, she would happily go to their 'hops' at Wesley or Sandford.

After secondary school, she had attended Miss Galway's Secretarial College and her first job was with a solicitor in Baggot Street, who used to chase her around his desk. Her equally beautiful older sister, Madge, had got a job in Lemons' Sweets and pulled her and a cousin who lived with them in behind her. She would tell us often that if they were late for the bus in the morning and the charmed driver saw them running down Whitebeam Road in their heels, he'd hold the bus till they got on and gasped their thanks.

Seani would teasingly note from behind his paper that the bus driver was probably the only Mick or Paddy that mammy seemed to meet.

If she wasn't sewing or knitting or washing or cooking or laughing, then she was reading. She had loved Jane Austen, Thackeray and Daphne du Maurier as a girl and that had matured to slightly more racy period romances like the ones written by Georgette Heyer. On the ground at her side of the bed, there was a stack of books with covers showing anguished looking heroines seated in front of their dressing-table mirrors, while tanned masculine hands rested proprietorially on their bare shoulders, fingers spread and seeming to reach downwards to where swelling bosoms spilled out and over the empire necklines of their dresses.

She read these and lent them to Mary or Margaret or Joan or swapped them back into Tony Clarke's shop to be credited against the next batch he'd assemble for her to buy. That was her own little refuge, till the years passed and she noticed a sudden interest on my part in these books about passionate governesses torn by their feelings for the widower fathers of their charges. She noticed that my interest in the books as bedtime reading material seemed directly proportionate to the cleavage displayed on the cover by the confused governess and both, in turn, seemed directly related to the contemporary and gradual transformation of the sheets on my bed from soft fabrics to something akin to plaster board. Just like that, in the wank of an eye, the beloved period romances with titles like *The Falcon and the Tit Willow* disappeared to be replaced by a stack of hard-boiled American homicide detectives created by Lawrence Sanders and Ed McBain, with covers showing blood-stained ice picks or tagged-toes on a mortuary slab.

As McBain would have put it, she was a 'stand-up girl'; she didn't go running to Seani about internal disciplinary issues. She took care of those herself and with alacrity, nor did she believe that it behoved a mother to explain her motives or why decisions had been reached. Her motto and the principle by which she raised her children could be summarised in either one of the two replies she would invariably give when interrogated by one of us as to why we had to do something: 'Because I said so', or the one that indicated that her fuse was lit and burning down quickly: 'That's the why'. Pursuing any matter past those explanations risked a raised hand, flashing eye and a mad footrace to stay ahead of her to the toilet door and locked sanctuary.

Her mother, my grandmother, was another Adelaide, and had a similar code of omerta about running to others with complaints or tittle-tattle. She was the source of my mother's 'knackiness' and craft with her hands and was summoned down from Dublin for any wallpapering or furniture-covering jobs where her daughter needed another pair of small-but-steely hands to close or pinch or gather. One visit from Granny Ad coincided with my first decision that, really, the whole 'school and me' thing was never going to work out.

Having to add or subtract at the blackboard in front of the rest of the class where they could see my stupidity was the sum of all my fears. Inspired by the way that people with colds were drawn in *The Dandy* and *The Beano*, I used one of my mother's lipsticks to polish my nose a shade that could have been scarlet but was probably closer to harlot and would have drawn a round of applause from Rudolph the Reindeer. Herself and himself took one look and agreed to keep me out of school till this terrible head-cold was gone.

I don't know whether Granny Ad was sympathetic or just picked up on my child-prodigy talent for deceit, but she gathered me in for a big comforting cuddle during which she smelt the lipstick. She dabbed her finger and tapped my nose twice before holding it under her own. Then she went back in to finish the cuddle. Never said a word. Never blinked an eye. Never turned a hair or turned in her spectacularly sly seven-year-old grandson.

Granny Adelaide's mother, my great-grandmother, was a Protestant who had converted upon marriage, and granny was raised Catholic under the *Ne Temere* doctrine. Her mother's family were called Lattimers, and they were the origin of this exotic German name, Adelaide. No-one or thing in Ireland was called Adelaide except for a road in Dublin upon which was located a hospital that was famously – and as far as my mother and grandmother's teacher nuns were concerned, disconcertingly-Protestant. Granny's family were bootmakers in the warren of streets around and behind Dublin Castle, a fact that was carefully concealed from Seani who would have heard 'bootlickers' for that occupation in that neighbourhood.

Both my grannys had been widowed early and had learned the hard way that, as the old saying had it, there were 20 shillings in every pound. That awareness of money and the need to manage it was transmitted to their children and notably to my mother. Both had a work ethic that was not so much imparted to them as molecular. She was all monetarist: spend only what you had and concentrate on the household as the basis for the wider economy. He was Kenysian: send the money around in a circle and give everyone a bang off it till it came back to him. But it had better come back to him, and it was her job to ensure that it did.

She kept Seani's accounts and happily played the miserly bookkeeper to his free-and-easy, 'Credit Terms Available' salesman. It was she who went out every two months to his bigger customers to get their accounts paid down, running a beady eye over their payments to ensure a workable balance between cash, reasonably safe first-party cheques and the risky third-party ones that the shopkeepers would try to move on to you. She loved the little battle of wits this represented and always cited the shop in Clare where she went in to be greeted by the familiar sight of a seven-year-old standing on a stool – not boiling milk this time – but manning the till in her daddy's shop.

Was the little girl's daddy in?

He was. What was he wanted for?

'I'm here to collect money', said my mother sweetly.

'I hope it keeps fine for you,' replied the little girl with a much, much older laugh.

She managed the household with an easy efficiency; bills arriving by post were opened and arranged in the order in which they were to be paid, before being wedged between a wall and the little transistor radio on which she listened to Gay Byrne and 'Dear Frankie'. Appliances were purchased from the ESB and paid down in instalments via a hatch in their Limerick shop. Any other major items were similarly bought and paid for. We must never owe a debt that kept us awake at night. It was always possible to pull your belt in a notch and squeeze through a week or fortnight and she was convinced that there was even a perverse enjoyment to be got from a concentrated scrimping if it meant that a threatening debt was paid. She was evangelical: we must manage our money, or it would manage us.

She was too convincing for her own good because I decided to take a much more direct interest in the state of my own finances. I had been given £16 for my First Communion in the old practically A5-sized green singles and brown fivers. In 1970 Ireland that was the deposit on a house.

In response to her airy suggestion-order ('I'll mind that money for you'), I happily handed it over. But a year later I was now ready to mind my own money. I wanted to let my belt out a notch or two: there were Airfix models to buy and Curly-Wurlies to eat; it was time to live a little. Where was my Communion money? She decided to brazen it out and told me that it was all gone.

'On what?' I demanded, suspicion and fury begin to surge like a jet engine.

Did I not remember the picnic we all went on to Curragh Chase, and the Taytos and Red Lemonade we'd consumed? She had used my money. That's where my Communion money had gone.

The first time that any Irishman of any age curses in front of his mother is a formative experience and so when my eight-year-old-self roared at her that we could have bought Taytos for all of fucking Ireland for £16, she wasn't feigning anger and horror; she was genuinely outraged.

She whipped out a clip to my ear and told me that I could forget about that money: even if it hadn't been spent on Taytos – which it had – it was now forfeit for the mortal sin of swearing in the presence of my mother. Manners would have to be put on me; they should have been put on me a long time ago and it was her fault they weren't because she'd been too soft. But they would be put on me forthwith. 'Indeed 'n' they would.'

I was genuinely incandescent at this brazen fraud and got into the habit of checking every pocket of all her coats daily for overlooked change or coins that I'd take by way of restitution. Every pocket of every coat, every day. Forget about buying a fridge from the ESB office on Cecil Street and Bishop's Quay, I was going to show her how a real instalment plans works. After weeks of systematic pilfering and diving my hands through balled-up tissues, I had enough to make a purchase symbolic of my commitment to restitution.

I ran down to the local shop and deliberately bought the most extravagant thing that any eight-year-old in Ireland in 1971 could imagine… a can of Coke. I opened it awkwardly, unused to the primitive finger-circumcising ring-pull, and then gulped it down vengefully dedicating every 'swally' to righting the wrong done to me and scanning the horizon for our grey Wolseley car with her embezzler's head just visible over the steering wheel. After drinking the 'tin of coke' I threw it down on the side of the road and stamped it violently flat in the manner that I knew the kind of teenage tearaways who habitually drank Coke did.

She hadn't noticed anything and couldn't prove anything even if she did notice. What was I doing watching the baddies on *Kojak* to try and pick up some tip? They'd nothing to teach me; if anything, they should be watching me if they wanted to learn something.

But she saw the empty crumpled can of coke on the side of the mile-long road between the shop and our house and – suspicions aroused – had deployed some crazy proto-algorithmam that through instant cross-reference to the age profile, gender, financial means and likely consumer tastes of everyone who lived on that stretch of road had worked out that it could only have been me.

I'm 58 now and I still don't know how from behind the wheel of a passing car she could have seen a flattened can on the side of the road and decided that I was responsible. But she did, and gave me a lifetime lesson that there was at least one person who I would never be able to fool or lie to or deceive. Because she knew – though some psychological or neurological or genetic hack – what I was going to think about something before I even knew I had started to think about *anything*.

She came through the door and announced casually that there was an empty can of Coke on the side of the road up from the shop. She doubted whether it was Mrs Alton (an Indian Army widow) or Mrs Gloucester (another merry widow with a pack of ravenous corgis and a jolly hockey sticks attitude to sherry and drink-driving). Both were ladies and would never be so common and uncouth as to drink directly from a can – much less while standing on the side of a public road. And she knew 'for a fact' that the Russell children or the Dunnes or the Hodkinsons or the Smiths were all too honest to be sneaking down to the shop with money they had stolen from their mothers' pockets.

Then the most beautiful pause followed by a public announcement that – so help her – if she found that 'anybody in this house' was going through the pockets of her coats in the wardrobe, then God help that boy.

She invested that warning with so much feeling and was so obviously 20 moves ahead of me that I lost my nerve and started to cry in front of her. I don't know if I cried a lot, but if I did it was more likely to be with rage than contrition.

I only remember her crying twice: once with fright when some sheets she had draped near the fire to dry during one of those interminable Limerick three-months-of-rain 'soft' winters caught fire and she had to bundle them all still burning out the window. Afterwards, she sat down, put her head into her hands and her shoulders heaved for a few minutes while we stood around her in a little circle asking her what was for dinner and when we could expect that to be served.

The only other time, when she took the phone call from Joan telling her that Margaret Russell had died, she groaned with grief and just couldn't stop. We were petrified because no-one had ever heard her distraught; it was unimaginable to any of us, to anyone that knew her. She only ever laughed or sang or told us that none of us were as good looking as our mother (true) or bust some *Age of Aquarius* dance moves and tell us that none of us could dance like our mother (true again) and that none of us had our mother's singing voice (at which we'd all chorus back… 'And thanks be to God for that').

I have adored her since I could fit my fat little hands around her ankle 55 years ago. Most of the things that I like about myself I'm pretty sure I got directly from her. I've never met anyone that laughed as much or made other people laugh as much as my mother. Even when the laugh was on you, you couldn't help but laugh with her. She once told self-conscious teenage me that my head was too small for my frame, and that I had a head like a peanut. She was right: my head was and still is too small for my frame and we both knew it. But only people that really love each other can say those things and not trigger some kind of nervous collapse, and we both knew that as well. Every time I catch a glimpse of my peanut head in a mirror, I laugh again.

And I will laugh at it till my time comes.

Her time must be very close now; Lady Feck-Mucky's carriage awaits. If she leaves the way she lived, she'll tell us that she's sick and tired of putting up with this feckology and that she has to make something beautiful to wear for when she meets all the others. She'll say that she has the pattern.

She's always had the pattern.

(Lady Feck-Mucky passed away peacefully on March 24, 2022, in her 90th year)

3

Feck the Halls…

A Child's Christmas Amongst the Gaels

ON THE LAST Sunday in November, my mother made the Christmas cake and pudding; I don't know why she went to the trouble, no-one particularly liked them. But she made them every year and she insisted that everyone took a turn stirring the heavy pebbledash mixture of sultanas, spices, sherry and nuts. We could make a wish while we did that. I always wished that someone would invent a different Christmas cake with less fruit and more cake. And I would always sneak in a related sub-wish that our relations in Cork wouldn't send us up one of those huge caraway seed cakes.

It had moved past bemusement to bitter resentment that on the one occasion in the year when eating cake was not just tolerated, but a religious duty, that neither of the two cakes in the house was appealing. The Christmas cake and pudding were for decoration, not consumption.

They were seasonal props, a baked equivalent of tinsel or the tree. They hung around like guests that had outstayed their welcome till mid-January when she would mill them between her hands back into the individual ingredients and leave them out on the lid of the USA

Assorted biscuit tin, for all the little birds that flocked around her like Saint Francis of Assisi, when she went out to hang washing on the line.

The caraway seed cake was a different affront in that it was neither decoration nor consumption. Where had it come from? And why? You never saw pictures of Ye Oldde Christmase Feasts where rosy-cheeked diners clapped with delight and toasted the arrival to the table of a cake the size of a cartwheel made of compressed budgie feed. But apparently no Cork Christmas was complete without one, which meant that every year my aunt and uncle in Cork – mindful of their brother's Siberian exile in Limerick an hour up the road – commissioned a baker in Macroom to hoard enough seed to panic the parrots in Madagascar and bake a cake the size of a foot pouffe, which they posted to him so as to arrive in the last post before the holiday.

One year the cake was so big that the postman put it on its side and rolled it up to the door with the bottom of his foot, the way the Guinness lads did delivering their kegs to pubs. Conscious of the effort and expense involved, Seani had to pretend to like it and nagged us all to try it… 'How do yee know yee hate it, if you've never tried it?'

I gave in once, when I was about 12, and told him to 'go on so' and cut me a slice. He began sawing down into it. He stopped to take off his jumper and when he resumed, little grunts of exertion were coming out of him. After what seemed minutes, he was up to his shoulder in the cake. He cut me a wedge the size of an aeroplane chock that I could not get into my mouth. 'Eat into it, and then up', he helpfully explained.

The two of us had sat facing each other with fine big mugs of tea. I began eating in and up, and adding big slurps of tea trying to chew the tasteless mulch down into a porridge that I could swallow. After a full two minutes, I realised that so far from getting easier to chew and swallow, the mixture was setting in my mouth like dental cement. It was getting harder and my own boyish jaws were getting weaker. I went up to a chew-speed that I wasn't to hit again till I started taking ecstasy, but the sliotar-sized ball of mulch in my mouth wouldn't reduce and was now settling perfectly over my windpipe.

I began to panic and, standing up, tried to get my fingers into my mouth and around it. But I couldn't, there wasn't room.

Seani, sizing up the situation, stood up, caught my hair, and turned my reddening face to his own. He peered in, flexed his fingers and in that cobra-like strike and withdrawal that he normally reserved for his wallet and cash transactions, he was in and out of my gob with half the mouthful of cake. I got the rest out myself and then burst into tears

It was the best Christmas ever.

Other Cork delicacies were also sent to us, and more gratefully received. There would be a carboard box with a slightly moist bottom where the glassy-eyed dead goose stuffed within had oozed a little. There would be spiced beef and invariably there was an exotic little box of Hadji Bey Turkish Delight, where the most famous delicacy produced by centuries of Ottoman sophistication and intercultural culinary experimentation had arrived in Cork and immediately been perfected. One visit, we were driving down McCurtain Street when Seani pointed out the shop where the sweets were made.

'Hadji Bey et cie'[2] we read aloud.

'What does *cie* stand for, da?' He told us to note the proximity of the train station further along. Not content with running trains and buses, he explained that CIE had diversified into making oriental sweetmeats using their mastery of the science of viscosity that both activities demanded. Perfect train axle grease was jellied and achieving that perfect consistency between solid and liquid was a transferable skill. That was why Hadji Bey had gone into partnership with CIE to make Turkish Delight.

---

[2] **Abbreviation of 'et compagnie': 'and company'**

The more he thought about it, the more convinced he was that it should be a matter of national pride.

'I bet you the Turkish Railways company couldn't make Shandons' Clove Rocks or Cleeves' Toffees. It's what I'm always telling ye… there is nothing holding the Irish back except ourselves ('And drink!' interjected my mother with sarcastic enthusiasm). Look at the job we've done on their best sweets, but there's no-one in Turkey making Peggy's Legs', he ended triumphantly.

A silence followed; he was in dead earnest when he said there was nothing holding us back only ourselves. It was indeed something he said often. But then he started smiling, then laughing gently, then laughing till his eyes filled up with tears and he'd to slow down because he couldn't see the road. When he was challenged on this explanation and accused of telling 'rowlers' and being a fibber, he pinched the tears out of his eyes and began urgently pointing out other landmarks to distract us.

The house always seemed much bigger at Christmas. Mostly because the best room in the house was opened for just those 12 days. Every other day, the Good Sitting Room was not just closed, but locked and barred to all except 'visitors', a complicated category that really meant people who didn't visit. The people who called in every day were categorically not visitors. My mother's best pals, Joan, Mary, and Margaret, who each visited twice daily on some unknowable rota, were just 'calling in'. That did not constitute 'having visitors' which was an altogether more formal matter. If a visit was important enough to warrant the opening of the Good Sitting Room, then everything else to do with 'having visitors' had to be upgraded to 'good': tea sets, shine on the furniture, shine on the girls' hair, cakes, clothes, biscuits, brasses, tray, posture and manners. Cushions had to be plumped, sandwiches had to be thin. The slightly stilted formal occasion that resulted, complete with traditional conversational themes ('What class are you in now?') and unforgiving evaluation of the host housewife's adherence to protocol, meant that 'having visitors' was the Irish equivalent of a Japanese Tea ceremony.

A few days before Christmas Eve, the Good Sitting Room was ceremonially opened to be aired, Hoovered, polished and possibly have the chimney swept. That opening was the signal that it was now so close to Christmas that we children could tell each other that we wished that it were Christmas without my mother gently interrupting and plaintively asking us to stop wishing our lives away. Her days were a blur of work and running around, and getting and going.

On the accepted basis that anything to do with the house and children was her job, all the presents and chocolates and wrapping were bought by her and carefully stowed at the back of her wardrobes. One December, when I was about eight or nine, I was going through the pockets of her coats looking for money, when I stumbled through into the Narnia Noel behind. By the time Christmas came, I had opened all the boxes of chocolates and eaten the bottom trays before forensically re-sellotaping. The Ker-plunk and Battling Gladiators had been taken out, assembled, played with, disassembled, and put back. The bottles of ginger ale had been wriggled downwards and out of their carry-packs immaculately without leaving so much as a crease in the cardboard, then half-drunk and refilled with a mixture of tap water and malt vinegar.[3]

We drove out to Murroe or Montpellier to cut holly and tear strands of ivy off the walls of sheds and from underneath corrugated iron roofs where it had crept. Those were draped over bannisters, around mirrors and along mantlepieces. Fresh straw had to be obtained for the crib in which the figures, like the costumed cast of a Hollywood biblical epic, waited for the infant lead's arrival on set from his trailer. Oasis foam was soaked

[3] Why just the ginger ale? Because via television dramas I understood that ginger ale went with brandy or cognac and, though we always had bottles of Hennessy, nobody ever asked for it. Even in a society as soaked in alcohol as that Ireland was, drinking brandy was considered risky. In a pub it would raise eyebrows, in someone's house it always raised voices and frequently fists. Seani, who was himself a solid pint-drinker, considered a full brandy glass to be the most dangerous balloon since the Hindenburg.

overnight and used to hold 'arrangements' of cones, ivy, little plastic deer, robins and snowmen all gathered nervously underneath wobbly, tall, red candles. Wooden wise men and their camels padded along the sideboard now bursting with new, eager, bottles of Harveys Bristol Cream and Sandeman Port that formed a front-rank screening off the old lags: rows of dusty unopened bottles of Harveys Bristol Cream and Sandeman Port. Behind them were other dustier bottles of Hennessy and Crème De Banana, Tia Maria, and, slightly apart, the other two old timers that sounded like they might have played for Italy in 1970 or be running Guatemala for the CIA and United Fruit, Cinzano Bianco and Martini Rosso. Grog ghosts of Christmas past. Bottles that had once, like the newbies, arrived all confident and shining, eager for the glass, but were now forgotten and resigned to the fact that their musty shelf was the only clink they would ever experience.

Deck the halls was an all fecking hands-on-deck affair: everything that moved was doing something, everything that didn't move was done. Jobs were delegated and strict timelines for completion understood. After the two days of cleaning and polishing and rubbing and shining, when all was in place, my mother herself flew the last mission around the house, taxiing out of the kitchen and taking off like one of the jets in Vietnam we saw on the news. She held an aerosol of silver paint at the end of one extended arm and an aerosol of artificial snow at the end of the other. My oldest sister flew wingman with a more modest payload of a carboard sheet. Siobhan would peel-off and go in first, banking steeply to place the sheet behind an 'arrangement' or some jungle of ivy and holly before climbing upwards and out of harm's way. Lady Fecky would adjust her approach angle, like one of the F4s and then taking careful aim, unleash with both barrels, spraying the target with artificial snow and silver paint, before pulling up, back to cruising altitude, while Siobhan retrieved the sheet of cardboard and they swapped the co-ordinates of the next target.

By teatime on Christmas Eve, the household was like a runner falling across the finishing line. Coal scuttles full. Ham boiled. Vegetables peeled and steeping in pots. Trifle setting. Flimsy sets of Chinese Christmas lights disentangled and cannibalised into one working set that didn't blow every fuse in the house when it was plugged in. Last minute visitors and presents received and reciprocated. Clothes ironed for the next morning, shoes polished. Hot water tank filling and heating. Bath numbers allocated, and notices of inspection issued.

The Christmas baths were our most important wash of the year and your place on the list depended on the priority our mother attached to you looking and feeling spotless, and her ruthless calculation on whether more dirt was being removed than was being added. In practice this translated to oldest girl first, then the next girl, then the youngest girl before concluding with Gunga and myself facing each other and speculating angrily about why the water was still so warm and whether the bubble bath had been added to disguise a giveaway yellow tint.

Afterwards, we would sit in our clean pyjamas and watch something like *The Great Race* or *High Society* while exchanging winks, micro-nods and tiny head shakes that decided who was going to see whether my mother's normal stop-and-search policy on crisps, sweets and biscuits had been suspended for the Christmas Season yet. She always did park it up for the 12 days, but the concession was never announced, so there was no way of knowing that you could help yourself to a packet from the Christmas Box of Taytos till someone got up the nerve to do just that without themselves meeting a crisp: 'And where do you think you're going with those? Put them back where you got them, and fast.'

At some moment that it seemed only he could intuit, my younger brother, Gunga, would get up and wander over to the Christmas box of Taytos to – as you hear it described now – call her on it: he'd make her make the decision.

He'd go into that box like a bear after a bun, noisily ripping it open and throwing bags of Taytos back over his shoulder to the grabbing hands behind. He knew that wherever she was in the house, even if she was out of earshot, even if she was on the roof, on some primal animal level she would 'feel' the change in vibrations, pick up on the charge in the air, and come to check out what was happening.

Which she duly did. Suddenly materialising in the doorway in the same vaguely supernatural way she suddenly materialised in any doorway to any room at any time when you were doing something or even thinking about doing something that she didn't want you doing. But then she would see the back of his little dressing gown bent over the box of Taytos and silently move back out of the door without challenging. That meant that the truce had started and for the next 12 days you could announce that you were having trifle for breakfast and, instead of responding with her customary 'Indeed 'n' you are *not*!' she would just sigh and warn us that not alone would we not have a tooth in our heads, but that it would serve us right.

We were put to bed early on Christmas Eve because meeting or even being awake when Santi arrived meant the whole arrangement was null and void. So, it was the only night in the year when we – or at any rate, I – went to bed early and uncomplainingly. Not even considered was Midnight Mass where the kind of fellas who drank brandy and who, Seani noted darkly, probably didn't attend 'Church, Chapel or Meeting Place' in the normal course of events, huddled at the back of the church, swaying, holding each other up and belching along to *Adeste Fideles*.

Lady Fecky, my mother, after days of endless jobs and domestic mullocking, still had to get all the presents for the five children out of a wardrobe, wrapped and down around the tree. Everything was tucked in under the tree.

We obviously knew all about the 'fill-the-stocking' thing; but not having those multi-coloured voluminous Pippi Longstocking Scandinavian or German varieties, we didn't think it was worth bothering with. What was going to fit into the standard Irish winter sock except those legendary single tangerines or solitary Brazil nut, the only gifts given to our forefathers who were invariably 'bloody glad' to get them? Irish feet and shins were just too small for us to run the risk of being fobbed off with the kind of presents that would fit inside their corresponding hosiery. No thanks.

The next morning, Christmas Day, began and proceeded in transcendent happiness. We went into Fecky and Seani's bedroom and woke them up so that we all went down to the Good Sitting Room together. The presents were opened and, babbling with joy, we started on what builders would call 'the first fix': opening the boxes and laying out the contents but not beginning assembly. We stopped to eat our fry and got ready to head off to Mass, slipping easily into our best clothes and shiniest shoes where they had been laid out the night before. When Mass ended, Lady Fecky and Seani wished all the other adults a happy Christmas while we breathlessly told our friends about our presents on the way up to look at the near life-size crib and say a prayer before returning to the house and girding ourselves for an even more sacred ritual.

The household's crate-sized Bush television was ceremoniously lifted from its normal position as the tabernacle of the ordinary sitting room and borne into the Good Sitting Room by Gunga, Seani and myself. Gripped with a white-knuckled intensity, it was moved carefully through the house like one of those Spanish processions where a revered Madonna is lifted out of her normal place and paraded around the town by devotees. We even stopped every few shuffled steps like they did, but only because my mother had read somewhere that the tube inside the set would explode if moved too fast. Timing was a factor here because the procession had to be completed and additional minutes allowed for the television to 'heat up' so that all was ready for the live broadcast of *Urbi et Orbi*, the Apostolic Blessing delivered from the balcony in Saint Peter's in Rome.

We were always encouraged to pause and listen to what was plainly intended to serve the same calming, reflective role as the Queen's Speech did for the British. That noble intention was not so much undermined as vaporised by RTÉ's routine habit of following it immediately with a broadcast of the annual visit to Cappagh Hospital by the cast of *Wanderly Wagon* accompanied by The Indians.

Wanderly Wagon was a popular children's programme set in a traditional horse-drawn barrel waggon with characters by Eilis Dillon and storylines by Frank Zappa. The other part of the wagon train out to the wild west of Finglas, The Indians, were a showband who wore feathered headdresses, warpaint and buckskin pants and arrowed in at number three in the list of great tributes to Native American culture, just behind smallpox and the mass extermination of the buffalo.

Cappagh was a children's orthopaedic hospital run by the religious and this annual televised encounter could stand for the strange mixture that was the 'Irish Christmas of the 70s', a half-creed of religion and standard western consumerism, nodding to both but belonging to neither. The cultural gears never grinded louder than those Christmas Day broadcasts from wards full of bedbound child patients, often encased in full body casts, trying to raise their heads off their pillows so they could see through the struts and screws of their skull braces to where Big Chief Empty Flagon was miming along to *Wig Wam Bam*, bouncing from foot to foot in his gift shop moccasins while beaming nuns clapped along.

Sweet Jesus.

The Christmas dinner was the standard but delicious orgy of different meats and mushy vegetables, with a notable patriotic twist being provided by the (even to us) bewildering number of variations on the theme of potato. In addition to boiled, roasted, croquettes, and mashed, we also had two more Cork specialities, potato sauce and potato stuffing. We ate the four types of cooked potatoes accompanied by a potato stuffing and covered with a potato sauce in that Irish way where food is something to be got through on the way to somewhere more interesting and amusing.

I'd say at our most leisurely, from the time we pulled our chairs in and said Grace, there wouldn't have been 10 minutes to the point where we pushed our chairs back and slowly waddled our individual way back into the Good Sitting Room where we pinched ourselves in a losing struggle to resist falling asleep and into a carb coma. Having spent three days tuning-up for the three-hour symphony of boiling and steaming that preceded the 10-minute performance, Lady Fecky had to spend the next two hours putting it all away and washing and folding and steeping and balancing all the various foods precariously on top of each other in the small fridge or in the colder rooms.

As everyone had fled before they could be asked to help, and in the humour for some company, she might play her beloved Johnny Mathis *Sounds of Christmas* album while she worked. When you levered yourself off the couch and went out for a Jimmy Riddle or the first futile attempt at the Christmas Tom Tit, you could hear her sing along to *Have Reindeer, Will Travel* or Johnny's version of the old Judy Garland classic *Have Yourself a Merry Little Christmas.*

Freed by the absence of the domineering television, our ancient Pye radio stereo seemed to flourish and flex itself to fill the vacuum, to swell the sound and show what we were missing when we insisted that it, too, defer to the household God. For the duration of Christmas and when my mother was in there, music filled the sitting room at real volumes – or at least as real as the old valves allowed. Sinatra, Count Basie, Sarah Vaughan, Dean Martin, Tony Bennett, Ella Fitzgerald.

She loved music and they both enjoyed the great American musicals with the exact mixture of fandom and fantasy they were meant to inspire. We had all the soundtracks to all the films of all the shows. When she was finished cleaning up after everyone else, she'd come in and sit down in her chair on the other side of the fire to enjoy the sequence of musicals being shown.

My younger sisters would squeeze in behind her, and Gunga might squeeze in behind Seani, where they all sang along to *The Street Where You Live* from *My Fair Lady*. Or cried when Nancy was killed in *Oliver* and congratulated the terrier on leading the coppers back to his brutal master, Bill Sikes ('Go on, Bullseye. I'd say that dog could talk to you'). Or poured every ounce of emotion they could muster into Seani and Lady Fecky's courting song, *Ever Loving Adelaide* from *Guys and Dolls*. Or laughed in amazement that anyone called Kelly considered it remarkable to sing and dance in a drop of rain that, by Irish standards, wouldn't warrant taking the washing back in off the line.

They sang their way through the afternoon and around the Midwest States, promising to meet me in Saint Louis and admitting to being as corny as Kansas in August, before switching states and chorusing the crescendo to Oooooooooooooo-klahoma with a snap that would have had Rogers and Hammerstein purring. They glowed with the happiness that singing brings, till there was a bright golden haze on the window.

The Angelus sounded the bell for routine, and both Seani and Lady Fecky disentangled themselves from sleepy draping children's arms to say their prayer and ready themselves to hear Maurice O'Doherty or Charles Mitchel give the news. She sat sideways with her back against the arm of her chair to listen, but he always sat up and leaned towards the television as if to signal to the newsreaders that they had his undivided attention. If he was going to hear bad news (and that's all we ever did hear) then there was no point hearing it slouched or slumped. It was the news' job to make you slouch and slump; if you were already slouched and slumped, you'd nowhere to go.

In the split-second after the last mournful 'BONG' of the Angelus and before the urgent music that announced the news, he always crossed himself, fixed his tie knot and smoothed his hair as if the television on which we looked at them had some secret two-way capacity that allowed 'them' to see 'us'. He always did it for the news. I'd love to be able to say that it was just a harmless psychological tic, but I worry that it could be genetic: his mother, our grandmother (who, on some worrying Bates Motel level, he insisted we also refer to as 'mother') used to close up her shop early and change into her very best clothes and shoes to sit down in smitten widowed silence to watch Dr Richard Kimble in the original television 60s series *The Fugitive*.

The other reason why Seani might have been paying such close attention to the Christmas Day news broadcasts was the popular national suspicion that 'on the day that was in it' a certain level of official tolerance was extended to newsroom staff having a little nip of the hard stuff as compensation for drawing the short straw in the Christmas roster. If that was the case, then more power to their pouring elbow: no-one could have begrudged them a quiet drink on the one day in the year when they didn't have to begin the bulletins by announcing that someone had died in a hail of bullets that day in Belfast or Strabane or Lurgan or Coalisland. Or, following an explosion, was currently being retrieved from the higher branches of the trees in Pomeroy or Portadown or Carrickmore, or any of the other northern places that were more familiar to our ears than the name of the roads in our local housing estates. By custom, a Christmas Truce was announced by 'P. O'Neill' and the 100-odd hours involved seemed the only days of the year when the immutable deadening sequence that had The Angelus, the music that announced RTÉ's evening news, and then the calm recitation of who had been killed earlier that day 'after answering his front door' or after 'an undercar device exploded', didn't apply.

We heard those Christmas news broadcasts in the same way as Sherlock Holmes heard the dog that didn't bark; it was the absence that revealed itself as the central component. The guns that didn't fire and the bombs that didn't detonate. The people that didn't die. Perhaps disorientated by the lack of the usual body count out of the north, 'ordinary' deaths by chip pan fire or car crash were reported and received almost giddily and the newsroom's heartfelt wish that you continued to enjoy your Christmas ended on the same cheerful note.

At around seven, my mother, Lady Fecky, was woken up and dispatched back out to the kitchen to make the sandwiches that was supper. She brought back in pots of tea and large serving dishes of ham sandwiches that were sent into whatever little crevices were still unfilled by the day's industrial consumption of food. After slogging our way through those, the table was cleared for own unique parlour game where my mother systematically destroyed any guide to the boxes of sweets or chocolates and then brutally applied the house rules that allowed you three seconds to pick one out while the other six people screamed at you to make your mind up before she moved the box on to the next, who was screeched at in turn.

Before she married, she had worked for Lemon's Sweets and their box was given a prominence that we didn't feel was merited by the contents. Cork's retaliation for the Fall of Constantinople, Hadji Bey Turkish Delight, was next up and savoured. Boxes of Quality Street, Roses, Milk Tray and Black Magic were eaten as if in a frenzy, with the general hilarity being added to by the series of pratfalls and fumbles I had to execute to 'accidentally' drop the boxes of sweets and disguise the fact that I had already eaten the lower trays because my life wouldn't be worth one of the despised orange liqueur barrels if that was discovered.

If Christmas afternoon was a musical journey around the American Midwest of MGM's backlot, then the evening television was always coffee at eleven and a stroll around Stephen's Green. We all joined in again for the inevitable rendition of *Dublin Can Be Heaven* with Noel Purcell and spat out our chocolates laughing at the undertaker's expressions on Maureen Potter and Danny Cummins as they skipped, dipped and flounced their way through their brilliant ballroom dancing sketch. The moment they struck some paso doble pose, the whole country received the same subliminal message and asked where the box of Double Centre chocolates was, and that and the boxes would be sent around again.

Wrecked and stuffed, people would start drifting off to bed shortly after. Some capacity had to be retained because there were 11 more days of this to be enjoyed. Not me. I always stayed right to the end. I would watch the traditional late film *Some Like It Hot* right to the end with my tired eyes refreshed by Marilyn's sheer black dress, and for the chance afforded to ask Seani about his mysterious relation who had narrowly averted being lined up against the wall with his pals from the Northside Gang in the massacre witnessed by Jack Lemon and Tony Curtis.

4

The Devil Wears Farah

THERE WAS NO uniform at Sexton Street. But the Brothers made it understood – through their patented method of delicate Feis Ceoil enunciation and bubbling pressure cooker menace – that their pupils, 'our boys', were expected to dress neatly and in a manner that indicated that they didn't intend giving the Brothers any 'gyp' on the three-year hoike to the Intermediate Certificate exams. After that first State sifting, there would be a mass bale out into various apprenticeships leaving a core group to undergo the more academically arduous – and perceptibly more middle class – 'to-Hell-and-back' two-year campaign to the Leaving Certificate, then quite a respectable qualification and possession of which, and not in completely remote parts either, was taken as denoting 'a scholar'.

For some reason, hints of which are still emerging, the Brothers seemed very concentrated on the type of trousers we were to wear. And in fairness to them, the 70s were a very fraught age where trousers were concerned. There had been the half-mast, tartan-seam abomination invented by the Bay City Rollers and perfected by their teenage girl fan base and Belfast's sectarian 'Prod' street gangs that involved a lot of flapping material around the shanks and which funnelled cold air upwards with a velocity that meant the freshest genitalia and coolest sperm since the Ice Age.

Striding forth alongside the half-mast, tartan-seamed flares but riding higher in the sartorial stakes were the cleaner-lined 'Spanish bags' which were the council estate version of the famous 'Oxford bags' and more Old Trafford than Old Eton. Spanish bags had a three-button, tie-over, cloth belt that was presumably designed to give some kind of matador's nipped waistline and they exploded outwards immediately below the scrotum into vast loon nylon legs that caught every delicate little zephyr and puff and bulged accordingly, so that even the most gentle breeze left wearers looking and sounding like the Cutty Sark going around Cape Horn in a Force 10.

The Brothers probably approved of the air-cooling capacity of these designs on little engines that were prone to the kind of overheating that might necessitate excessive manual venting. But the Oxbridge connotations – communism, treachery, rugby, homosexuality, intelligence – made these trousers, or any such voluminous variant, suspect. It could never do to have the clean limbs of Irish boys tented in these kinds of fey pantaloons. No. On the matter of trousers, the Brothers were unambiguous. The trousers should be grey and made of flannel. Their ankle width should not differ widely from their calf width.

A pause here... and a meaningful stare over the bifocals.

He was reliably informed that Moran's in William Street sold trousers that the boys' mothers might like to consider. They were suitable in every respect and were reasonably priced. A last 50,000-watt glare around the room to make sure that the order had been understood and then the resumed carefully enunciated instructions.

The Brothers themselves were generally serious and effective teachers with personalities that ranged the full gamut from decent to demonic. Brother Hogan taught Latin and English and, it was whispered, had arrived in Sexton Street direct from some military academy in Bulawayo where he had translated the *Gallic Wars* into Shona and taught candidates for the elite Selous Scouts a variant of panga (machete) slashes, hamstring slicing and blocks based on the Tipperary hurling of his boyhood. He was reputed to be a crack shot and to be able to top a boiled egg with a Lee Enfield at a hundred yards.

We learned a standard, formal English in which much emphasis was placed on grammar, composition and the correct command of syntax. Brother Hogan moved with that peculiar lightness that porky people often possess, and spoke softly and with a perfectly even tone. He didn't have to raise his voice because if his lips even twitched, a terrified silence descended, and heads craned to catch every syllable.

Everything he said mattered and we understood almost instantly that the volume with which Brother Hogan spoke, or the stress he laid upon certain words, were not reliable indicators of the weight of his concern.

He had a little herd of collective nouns he disliked intently ('a lot of '... 'a load of') and would raise his cold eyes and entreat us not to insult him, or the vocabulary we should all at this stage possess, by their usage. Very detailed instructions were given out with his Friday afternoon essay title about sentence structure and sub-clauses, and he would end with a smile and a droll request that we might be so good as to give a margin of a single, imperial inch for his comments.

Three days and 30 raw hands later, you realised that it was that last chuckled throwaway that was the most important thing. He had measured every margin and identified those that were not exactly one inch. He showed us the wooden ruler that was the one he favoured when he was measuring an inch. We might like to invest in one of this type, he helpfully suggested to the lads sitting with their pulsating red hands clamped between their Farah-covered thighs for relief. Of course, we were free to buy whatever ruler we wanted and take our chances that it coincided with his calculations. His calculations were based on the type he was holding up now.

The title of our essay was to be underlined once and in blue ink.

Once. And in blue ink. Not red ink. Not black ink. Blue ink. The kind of blue ink that came out of a biro such as the one he was holding right now. He believed it was manufactured by Messrs Faber. He knew for a fact that supplies of this type of pen were available in the school shop. Our copy books were not to be allowed become grubby or stained. He thought covering the essay copy books with wallpaper was a good idea so long as the boy's name was clearly legible. He didn't – he most certainly did not – want to be left searching for the name of the individuals whose essays he was correcting. That would constitute a waste of his time, which he valued greatly. He could not accept a situation where he would be trying to discern the name of the individual against some eye-jarring modern pattern or design, and straining his sniper's 20/20 to read some scrawl and if that meant a glued white paper panel superimposed on the wallpaper and bearing the name of the pupil, so much the better.

Did we all understand now what we had to do?

Nobody had any questions? Very good, then he would expect these very reasonable requests to be complied with properly.

The essays were handed in on Monday with Brother Hogan delivering his verdicts in Tuesday afternoon's class. The classes each side of our room would have been in session for five minutes or more before we would hear his sandals slapping their onomatopoeia way down the hall. The slapping sound got louder as he drew closer, till almost to our relief he would bank suddenly through the door and smoothly swerve left over to his desk on which he would carefully place his pile of essays, stand back and then run his index finger down the pile to some secret marker.

Keeping his finger on the marker, he would step back in and gently twist the pile so that the books on the top were now square on, while the books at the bottom were oblique. He would pick up the top pile and holding it against his chest begin skimming out the copy books of those boys who, he noted approvingly, were doing their work… were listening to him…were not wasting his precious time.

After the last copybook frisbee'd its way to the sweaty palm of its owner, there would follow one of those count-to-five, cold sweat pauses that are the mark of someone who really understands the art of terror.

'And now for the boys who aren't listening… the boys who didn't understand my requests last Friday but were too lazy to ask questions and find out what was required… the boys who are (a little doleful sigh here) wasting my precious time.'

I was good at English and think I only got leathered once. But there were lads who got it every week. And it wasn't a joke slap; this was serious if temporary pain inflicted through some fairly serious exertions. Weirdly, as I get older, I seem to resent more and more not the actual violence itself but the vicious ham theatricality of it all. It wasn't so much the welter of slaps and the precision lining-up of the hands. It wasn't even the hippo ballet that saw this little rotund, red faced man getting up on his tippy-toes to get that critical leverage for a proper arc and swing.

What I feared then and have come to hate was the ceremonial preamble. The studied, jaunty, whistling entry. The careful placing of the pile of copy books on the desk and the elaborate way he then twisted the pile dividing it into the sheep and goats, the saved and sinners. The mechanical way he flicked the good essays over our heads easily and at a constant speed, like they were clay pigeons, and the way he must have enjoyed watching all those young terrified eyes scanning the airborne traffic frantically for that familiar pattern, that cheap wallpaper from the parlour or the sitting room that just weeks ago they wouldn't have been able to describe if their lives depended on it, but was now, in that insanely terrible instant, the most important thing in their lives.

Of course, I've reason to be grateful to Brother Hogan. I know good

English when I read it and when I (increasingly infrequently) summon up the discipline needed to write it. I'm still able to strike that formal or semi-formal note that makes 'claims officers' hesitate before throwing a letter in the bin on the grounds that a person who seems to know – or is mad enough to be bothered – about paragraphs and punctuation might be able to make trouble, if so inclined. Was that worth having the shit scared out of you at 13 years of age? I don't know. Possibly. Probably.

I do know that 45 years later I can still remember the cold sweat gathering at the base of my 13 years old spine when Brother Hogan swept through the door and a Gilbert and Sullivan tune in my ears makes me want to George and Gilbert in my pants.

Light relief was provided by Brother O'Halloran, who taught Irish and whose galloping dementia meant that he could never remember who he had just decided to hit. In the same way as film directors 'story board' sequences, Frame One would see him assume a facial expression that conveyed a decision to give someone a slap. In Frame Two he would take a couple of big, mad, Groucho Marx steps that would have him beside the miscreant. Frame Three – he puts a finger to his lips to indicate that no-one was to talk and thus alarm the object of his rage, who he fondly imagined was completely unaware of the retribution about to be visited upon him. Frame Four – dives his right hand into his soutane and begins extracting rosary beads, wine gums, a sliotar, a penknife, quite possibly the chanter from some bagpipes, before eventually emerging, minutes later, with semi-tumescent leather. Frame Five – immediately changes his expression so completely that you knew he had forgotten why he was standing beside Terence McNamara. Frame Six – quickly re-packs his bric-a brac and, on the basis that no-one likes a wasted journey, vigorously lays into whoever was handiest and wearing an indictable amount of denim.

There was the youngish Brother Skehan from Dublin who, upon being asked whether it would be possible for us to play soccer during a P.E. session sweetly inquired the names of those individuals who preferred Luther's football to our own native games. There was a Brother Beery, nicknamed 'Steamer', a dangerous and sinister nonce, who would try and cut out boys from the crowd the way the sheepdogs did on Phil Drabble's *One Man And His Dog*. His hair was a shade of snot green where he ran his fiddler's maw over his nose and back over the comb-over.

There was Brother Ross the Head Brother who lost control of the school to the thugs. There was Brother Power, who won it back. Before either of them was the ferocious Brother 'Knacker' McGirl, whom I seem to recall as a Bishop Casey lookalike and who I once saw nearly box unconscious a boy who had spat on the ground in his presence. And there was Brother McSorley.

Brother McSorley was known as 'Spike' and taught science. To him fell the Sisyphean task of teaching us the Billings method of natural contraception. I can't remember how he explained it, but I seem to recall that before either you or the girl had taken off so much as your vest, certain calculations had to be made. For that purpose, we were advised to keep the following items handy (perhaps on the bedside locker or on a little ledge underneath the Sacred Heart) a thermometer, a calculus log book (where pi equals 3.14 to infinity), a calendar, a miniature torch... and there's some debate about whether a sextant was also required. That straightforward matter disposed of, Brother McSorley turned his attention to the two matters that exercised his passions most: the banning of Sean South from the national airwaves and the presence of graffiti on the desks of his science laboratory.

On our very first day in a science lab that Copernicus would have been able to find his way around, Spike ordered us all sit down. He then bustled his way around the room sliding off-cuts of timber in front of each of us (he was also the woodwork teacher. Why not?)

'Have you all got a bit of timber?'

'Yes, Brother.'

'I said... have you all got a bit of timber?'

'Yes... Brother.'

'Very good. On the bit of timber in front of you, write down your own name. Now write down the name of your girlfriend (is there something funny, Mr McNamara?).

Now draw a swastika.

Now write 'Man United are magic'.

Now write 'Slade rule OK.'

Now write 'Tin (sic) Lizzy. Have you all done that?

'I said... have you all done that? Yes? You've all done that?

'You have? Good... good...(a pause here to fill his lungs and summon the energy to scream)... NOW YOU WON'T HAVE TO DO IT ON THE DESKS!!'

Brother McSorley, and most of the other Brothers, spoke to classes or assemblies in that screeched, repetitive and sarky, question-and-answer style that the wider world only became aware of after they witnessed R. Lee Ermey's barnstorming turn as Gunnery Sergeant Hartmann in *Full Metal Jacket*.

'DID I TELL YOU THAT ESSAY WAS TO BE HANDED UP TODAY? I *DID* TELL YOU THAT, DIDN'T I? SO, I'M *NOT* A LIAR. WHAT'S THAT... I CAN'T HEAR YOU!'

Like the character Hartmann, McSorley urged upon us all the importance of developing a personal relationship with an issued weapon. Sextons was a hurling school. It had briefly flirted with soccer and won all round it in that code, but the pupils and supporters had been involved in several instances of serious crowd disorder that gave the suspicious Brothers their chance of banning this Saxon pestilence with its sideburned, Ford Capri-driving, Liverpool and Leeds heroes. The school returned to the pure Corinthian spirit that comes with putting a yard of ash in the hands of a teenage boy and telling him to stick to the lad he's marking like shit to a blanket, while cutting rashers off him if the sliotar comes within an asses' roar of either of them.

On the day of a Harty Cup match against some Cork crowd like North Monastery or Farranferris, Brother McSorley would solemnly open a special cupboard-come-armoury inside which was stored heavy five-foot-long staves and shovel handles bearing tiny little napkin flags in the school's colours. Anyone who fancied themselves queued up to be sized up by Brother McSorley and handed a suitable club. The brawniest and toughest need only apply; valuable poles were not to be wasted on young fellas who would hesitate to open one of the Cork skulls when the moment arrived. And yet some pretence had to be kept about the nature and purpose of the *levee en masse.*

So Spike would chant 'For waving' at every boy, even as he proffered the shillelagh.

'For waving… For waving... For waving…'

In this martial trance he would arm us all till the appearance of some insanely dodgy thug volunteer from the nearby Technical School would snap him out of his reverie.

'For waving. Get out! For waving. Who are you? For waving. Get out of my sight before I put my foot up your arse!'

I loved the communal pretence about the real purpose of the kendo stick-length poles and their teacloth sized flags. There was something very Catholic, very metaphysical, about it. If Thomas Aquinas was going to attack a busload from Knocknaheny with a five-foot long pole, this is how he would have rationalised it.

The matches were invariably held in out-of-the-way locations like Bansha, near Tipperary Town, or Buttevant, between Mallow and Cork city, where there was a bit of a green handy to the pitch and a conveniently small Garda presence. If Sextons lost the match, our Brothers would ostentatiously shake hands with their Cork counterparts, wish them well in their progress through the competition, before transmitting their dark wishes to the NCOs through furious stares and an indignant clamber into the monastery's Hillman Hunter or Talbot Solara that would carry them home to Limerick and away from the mayhem about to begin. Their car's disappearance out of sight was the signal for the first charge and whatever about the hurling, no-one could touch the Limerick boys for their ability to get seriously violent at the drop of a hat.

The school had a large sprinkling of country lads – indeed, they formed the backbone of the team – but the 'other team' was from the city estates that would later feature so prominently in the newspapers' crime reports and would become so lawless and degraded that their regeneration would become a national policy objective. The lads from these estates knew how to fight at a pitch of violence that I could not even have imagined till I witnessed it.

They learned the rudiments on the streets of poor districts like Weston or the Island Field or Southill and honed it down to a black perfection in the Market's Field of a Sunday when Shamrock Rovers, Dundalk or Waterford could be expected to give it a serious go.

My own idea of fighting involved getting your opponent in a headlock till his forehead became red and he gave up. The lads from the Island Field began every row looking for an opportunity to kick the enemy in the bollocks till he was doubled over, at which point the focus switched to the head. It was never nice to look at. And it was even worse to receive. But as a template for successful street violence it was itself impossible to 'bate'.

The brutal poverty that had sent half the city into TB sanatoriums or the graveyards with the other half heading off the Acton or Aston had long finished by the time I went into town for school. And we weren't poor at home; my dad had a decent wholesale fruit and vegetable trade, so we always had a bit of money and could buy what we wanted – within reason. Seani lodged every week and my mother did the accounts so that there was a cash flow that kept the household going.

Birthdays and Christmas presents were generously observed and went off without any hassle unless I was given a geometry set, in which case I would throw a strop that might last for days on the perfectly reasonable grounds that an opportunity to buy me something I actually wanted had been lost for the sake of something to do with school that they had to buy me anyway. The idea that you might have to do without something vital or not get enough food was, thankfully, unknown to me. I might have had some vague idea, a compound of little match girls, snow and a racking cough, but I had never witnessed people nonchalantly admitting that they had not been fed at home.

I had never heard tannoy announcements that openly instructed those boys that hadn't had a breakfast to queue for a cup of milk and a bun during the first break. I watched amazed as dozens of boys calmly queued up to accept the charity and I knew that these had to be genuine cases and that no-one was pretending for the sake of getting a free bun: the Brothers monitored the queue carefully and would be able to judge in a split second whether their bun was going to a genuinely empty stomach or whether the supplicant was just chancing his arm. In which case, he would discover that he had actually been chancing his jaw.

Every morning then saw us all converging on the school like the workers to a Lowry mill. The small boys in the primary school wore little grey duffel coats and leather caps with fastening straps that covered the ears, and they trotted alongside their older brothers sailing along in their wind-powered Spanish bags and flapping knee-length, wide lapel, double-breasted coats. The tipped brogues and loafers rasped the paths and concrete and the cherry docs splashed the grey canvas.

Even through the rose-tint of memory it all seems so grey. Grey morning sky, grey afternoon sky, slate grey blocks under grey slate roofs, black or denim jackets wreathed in grey smoke from the fags bought individually from Ballsy's shop.

Every shade in the rainbow of grey.

I'd hop out of my dad's truck down in Gerald Griffin Street and walk up through Tanyard Lane where the school's challenge fights or 'claims' were held. The lane apparently featured in an edition of the *Guinness Book of Records* for being the location where one of the largest rats on record had been captured. As the name suggested, the area was thick with tanning yards and at the top of the lane where it joined Mulgrave Street sat the squat old stone warehouse that sold animal feeds. The lads working there would stand in the grey sunshine smoking fags held with elbow length tough leather gloves to protect them from the nipping rodents.

Across the road was St John's Pavilion where to our immense pride, 'Tin' Lizzy, whose complicated geometric logo disfigured Brother McSorley's desks, had played in a gig promoted by a teacher in our school.

I suppose the school would have been considered rough and not the kind of place where you wanted to stand out for the wrong reason. The trick, as is always the case, was to blend in without being seen to be making an effort to do so. I had to move fast. I hadn't gone to the primary schools that the rest of the lads had attended and so far from having a proper Limerick accent, I had developed a Little Lord Fauntleroy accent and vocabulary through repeated readings of the *Just William* series of books and intense wide-eyed exposure to the likes of *Goodbye Mr Chips, Ice Cold In Alex* and all those Royal Navy recruitment movies that had an unflappable Noel 'mad about the buoy' Coward on the ship's bridge, while his destroyer pitched around the Ealing Ocean and cheerful cockney seamen ferried him up mugs of tea and openings for patriotic pronouncements.

When Brother Hogan called my name during the very first roll of my class, 1K and I called back, in my best 'Demn you, Jerry' tones something like 'Enn-show', the wolfpack heads broke the surface, extended themselves like periscopes and then slowly turned to face the target.

After a couple of weeks of healthy pulverisation, I made a very conscious decision to get with the programme and began making the key sartorial adjustments that signalled to the wolf pack you had at least clocked their look and realised how hopelessly deficient your own gear was.

That makeover had to be done very slowly, almost imperceptibly, or you ran the risk of being 'claimed' on your new look. Because if you wanted to look like them – and therefore escape their regular internal disciplinary vettings – then you had better be able to kick heads like them. And I wasn't. I hit instead on a dodgy Moonstomp-meets-Moonshadow vibe that had wrangler and tartan-lined bomber jackets up top and Cat Stevens and Jim Croce cords and cowboy boots underneath. It passed muster, but there was a pretty obvious each-way bet going on and my look always gave off that aesthetic white noise that radiates from clunky dual-purpose combos like amphibious cars or clock radios.

I decided to eliminate any possibly gay colours which left me with a grand total of three: black, grey and brown. Wearing all black was to write a tough guy cheque I was not able to cash. Wearing all grey in an Irish city of the 70s was simply to wear camouflage. I picked brown and started wearing a shirt, jumper, jacket, jeans and boots of microscopically different hues. I was very happy with the results till one day one of those whose ire the ensemble aimed at deflecting told me that I looked like a walking shit.

I gave a Diana Fossey level of focus and study to the way the alphas moved, stood, walked and smoked and then developed a more restrained middle class variant, a more 'May-one-ask-what-the-fuck-one-is-looking-at?' than the original.

Their walk was actually hard to get. You could categorise it as a Paddy pimp roll insofar as they all walked the same and it was such an unnatural gait that you had to make a conscious decision to walk this way. It was also like the pimp roll in that it was much more about the semiotics than the locomotion; the announcement being made than the amble.

It was sometimes laughed at as the 'Here's me head... and me arse is following' walk but you wouldn't generally be sharing the joke with the truck-and-trailer object of the sneer.

Its most defining characteristic was the three distinct hyperextensions involved: shoulders down and forward, head slightly further down and slightly further forward, with the forehead furthest out, like the battering ram on a trireme – which was indeed its purpose. (Your visual cue here would be *Alien* where the galactic lizard keeps on having smaller jaws shooting out of already extended jaws.)

Set thus, the upper body remained absolutely immobile. No swinging of the shoulders and, most definitely, no vestige of any kind of hippy bounce off the ball of the foot. Beneath the banked flesh-and-bone battlements of the thrusting head and down to the waist, nothing must move. Like a Rodin marble, the movement should be a promise, in this case the promise of physical pain. From the waist down, that stately superstructure gave astonishingly abrupt way to an almost manically fast snappy stride that flicked and turned the foot outwards at the end of every speedy step. It was a reverse Mason-Dixon Line that had the south all piston pumping industry and the north a kind of bellicose lassitude.

In those pre-Pit Bull days, the walker was very often accompanied by his 'tarrier', one of those legendary Jack Russell terriers, whose vaguely threatening demeanour and unfathomable basilisk eyes were the obvious inspiration for the whole look. You'd see them walking down William Street looking neither left nor right, eyes fixed on something – or someone – in the oblivious middle distance. Both affecting to not even be aware of the way that oncoming pedestrians stepped into the gutter or the sudden horn-honking, bumper-brushing, dashes being made through traffic to the other side of the street to avoid them.

These dogs of war processed like Prussian Guardsmen: perfectly synchronised step and eyes at 12 o'clock with that exact spirit level bubble divide between rigid uppers and frantic moving lowers. If you saw three of them going down the street abreast with their dogs and their invisible snare drum beating out their silent double-time, it was all you could do not to stand to one side and salute them passing.

You half expected the fucking Kaiser to appear on a shop canopy and point them towards Paris.

5

The Taste of Pandy and the Smell of Benji

SUNDAY MORNING ANNOUNCED itself with two competing sounds: the fry noisily sizzling in 'Cookeen' lard and my father's bath being run. The five of us were bathed the previous evening by my mother, Lady Fecky, in a split-second perfect ballet of bubbles and barked orders. She queued up the five and started undressing us at different speeds with the whipping off of underwear timed to coincide with our 'go'. When that came, we were lifted into the bath and received a gentle-but-irresistible press down as our delicate undercarriages hovered above the scalding water and our tearful pleas were rejected with a hangman's equanimity.

She kept the shoulder clamp for the minute it took for the panicky screams to subside and our little bodies to became acclimatised to the temperature and began splashing and playing. Pausing only to promise terrible retribution 'if so much as a drop of water' was spilt out onto the floor, she would dart back into the hall to work on the conveyer-line behind. When those four had all been moved onto their next individual stage and repositioned the way she wanted, she ghosted back in bath-side and blindside of the by-now laughing child, put a crane-grab hold on the head and used a cake mixing bowl to ferociously and repeatedly douse it from a height and with a force that would have turned the turbines out the road in the Ardnacrusha power station.

As the slightly stunned child, open-mouthed with disorientation, gripped the sides of the bath to prevent themselves slipping beneath the water, shampoo was fired in, worked furiously into a lather and immediately rinsed out by another waterwheel of bowls. A split-second pause to register whether the eyes still had soap in them, an adjustment of the bowl angle to horizontal, and then one single massive whoosh of water into the eyes and down the throat of the still open little mouth.

A firm grip under the arms that easily adjusted to a Heimlich manoeuvre[4] if a dangerous volume of water had been swallowed and then the child was lifted out of the room and maul-dried with a towel standing in the hall with particular violent attention paid to the ears, between the toes and the eyes and nose, where residual snot (nose) and cack (eyes) might linger. The same water did the five and in order of the perceived need for cleanliness, so eldest girl first, through the next two girls and onwards to Gunga and myself, who shared.

We didn't have a shower and didn't get one till I was 11. When we did it was so eccentric and the control dials so counter-intuitive and treacherous that even considering using it brought on the kind of cold sweat that compelled its usage. It was either hot-as-hell or as cold as a witch's tit, with no possibility of achieving any temperature in-between and the whole painful cruel episode most resembled trying to defuse a landmine on which you'd deliberately stood, in that you couldn't try and work it out without turning it on and then being alternately scalded and frozen. It defied us all and when my mother announced that she was going to write a letter of complaint to the manufacturer, my precociously foul-mouthed bother Gunga told her to include his conviction that 'a fucking

[4] Although I'd be pretty sure that if you'd asked anyone in 70s Ireland what the Heimlich manoeuvre was, they'd have guessed at a Robert Ludlum novel.

safecracker' wouldn't have been able to work out the temperature dial.

Eventually, through non-use and the virulent limescale associated with Limerick's hard water, it seized up completely, which is obviously what it wanted from the moment of its installation. Its malevolence meant that we were all still having shallow birdbaths or having to squat underneath a hand-held rubber hose attachment that fitted unenthusiastically onto the bath taps well into our teens, and having to do with the resultant hunkered low-pressure colonic irrigation instead of the confident obedient showers that everyone else seemed to be able to have.

Immediately after he ate his fry, my father hopped into the bath. While he was there, I polished the shoes; his, Gunga's and mine, and gave the girls' patents a rub of a waxy cloth. I loved seeing him out of his work clothes and in the grey or brown checked suits he preferred. He wore viyella shirts and bought a brand called Van Heusen, with the whole ensemble completed by a tie with a complicated knot that he told me was often mistakenly referred to as a Windsor. The real Windsor knot 'and don't forget it' was the noose that many a good Irishman had had tightened around his patriot neck.

He trusted his own sense of style and he was right; he was handsome with a crinkly Normal Mailer head of hair, and he scrubbed up well. His sartorial confidence took a bit of a dent when he came back one night and proudly showed us all an expensive shirt he had bought that day in a gentleman's outfitters in Tulla that featured a busy motif of earnest looking policemen on tandems. When this was pointed out, he laughingly assured us that they were only on the cellophane packaging.

His shock when he discovered they weren't just on the wrapping was profound and he completely lost confidence in his own judgement – never again wearing a stitch that 'mammy' hadn't selected and put through her own much more stringent due diligence process.

As a kind of aperitif, everyone got into their clothes for Mass to the sound of whatever religious service RTÉ radio was broadcasting. Once ready, we climbed into the car to wait for my mother who got in last after a high-heeled sprint from the front door and momentary pause to smooth and fold her skirt so that she didn't sit on it. She wore a silk scarf over her hair and clutched her 'good' bag in dainty and immaculate black leather gloved hands. Then it was only a case of deciding what Mass to nibble on from the dizzying eucharistic buffet available.

Our parish church was up the road in Monaleen, but it was just as easy to go down the road to Saint Patrick's or into Limerick proper to Saint Michael's or any one of the dozens of monasteries, priories or order houses at which the even-by-Irish-standards famously devout locals heard Mass. The Dominicans' priory of St Saviour's had a picture of Heaven that surmounted the altar with all the order's heavy hitters facing off on two opposing banks of cloudy benches, John of Cologne, Hyacinth of Poland, Thomas of Zumarraga, resplendent in mitres and impressively confident on their precarious cumulus couches.

If we kids were ever asked where we wanted to get Mass, we always chose the Dominicans because – in addition to the cotton wool cloudy portrayal of Heaven – there was a seriously good chance that the prayers and litanies would be interrupted by the sound of Sammy Benson's marching band striking up some brassy cha-cha-cha air directly outside in Tate's Square. I often wondered whether he was deliberately synchronising the brassy opening of a tune like *Brazil* with the solemnities within. But it must have been coincidental, no-one then would have had the nerveless timing to follow a Dominican intoning the Consecration, 'This is my body, which will be given up for you. Do this in memory of me' with an urgent quick-stepped version of the theme from *The Magnificent Seven*.

After Mass and a trip to the shop for the papers and sweets, my father dropped us home, to begin preparing dinner while he went to Fennessy's pub to begin his own holy trinity that involved visits to three different pubs to have a drink with three different circles of friends for three different purposes at three pre-ordained and immovable times. My mother would check on the leg of lamb put on earlier and begin peeling and boiling pots of vegetables to accompany it. We had an (even then) ancient Pye cabinet radio and turntable and she'd ask us to put on Ray Charles, Tony Bennett or Sinatra or, most often, her favourite, Johnny Mathis, and the potatoes, turnips and mushy peas bubbled along to *Warm* or *Chances Are* or *Baby, Baby, Baby.* I always noticed a little involuntary downward tug on my father's mouth if a Johnny Mathis record was on when he came back through the door from Fennessy's. Why, he would ask as he put down his keys, could we not listen to Irish singers.

Like who exactly? 'Like Orthurrr Tracy, The Street Singer', he'd reply, giving his favourite that respectful orotund pronunciation and full Tin Pan Alley title and ignoring the groans. Johnny was quickly pulled off and soon *Laughing Irish Eyes* or *Did Your Mother Come From Ireland* filled the house as Orthurrr (real name: Abba Avrom Tracovuksky) worked his Top O' The Morning tenor up to the Top O' The Scales. The near ultra-sonic whistled intro to *It's A Sin To Tell A Lie* had every dog within a five mile radius barking, and your teeth ready to explode. But my father would sit back, eyes closed in beatific contentment, his lips forming the words as he murmured along to all the songs, whether in the great Irish tradition of O'Edipus, *It's My Mother's Birthday Today* and *To Mother – With Love* or Orthur's hard-to-ignore preoccupation with gypsies: *Gypsy Fiddles, Dance, Gypsy, Dance* and *In A Little Gypsy Tea Room*, the spell only ending with the explosion of frenzied whisking that announced that the flourbergs in the gravy had been located and were being dealt with. Dinner was ready.

I didn't then, and still don't, understand why any kind of distinction was made between the different vegetables, either in terms of cooking or serving. Thirty seconds after the plate was put in front of any of us everything was worked and folded into a delicious buttery multi-coloured mound that we called Pandy, yet another example of Irish ingenuity that our Saxon foes had tried to appropriate by making it the surname of one of their television puppets who wore – insult to injury – a transplanted convict's striped suit.

Afterwards, the dishes were cleared, washed, dried and put away, the pots were filled with boiling water to steep, the sides of the good table were let down and it was restored to its workaday dimensions and lifted against a wall. Then the seven of us might crowd into the small sitting room and watch RTÉ's Sunday afternoon film in which some combination of Jeanette MacDonald, Johnny Weissmuller, Kathryn Grayson, Cheeta the chimpanzee, Nelson Eddy or Gordon McRae yodelled, trilled or cooed. Many of the films seemed to be set in an old Araby where some gender-reversed version of Sharia is in force: the women unveiled, tresses flowing, and visibly overheating despite the best efforts of the little black boy doing double-time on the ostrich feather fan, had peeled grapes dropped into their mouths by duskier looking slave girls, while apparently indifferent sheikhs, swaddled head-to-foot in white silk niqab with flashing eyes only just discernible, diverted their energy into suggestive acrobatic mountings and dismounts of their horses and elaborate triple-dip curlicue Salaams.

The other exotic of choice were the Mounties and their Canadian forests, Tarzan's jungle and Warner Brothers' oasis, and are now so hopelessly confused and the plots and cast so interchangeable in my memory that all have morphed into a mental reel in which Cheeta – in miniature Mountie uniform and hat – lies seductively on a mound of scatter cushions in an art deco Bedouin tent gazing rapturously at Gordon MacRae who's wearing chiffon harem pants, a hussar's jacket and a coonskin hat while they duet magnificently on *Indian Love Song*.

We would sit in the near darkness of a Sunday afternoon in late autumn or winter, transfixed by these visions of loveliness, hypnotised by the music, enthralled especially by the whiteness and perfection of the teeth. My mother would remark on how well they all kept their teeth.

When Cheeta gnashed his teeth and pounded up and down on the spot, she would note, ruefully, that even their monkeys had better dentists than us. Tranquilised by the yodelling and orthodontics, we stared at the small black-and white box, squeezed into the two armchairs or lying flat on our tummies on the floor, digesting and processing the boiled vegetables and mushy peas Pandy and nonchalantly parping out the resulting 'rude noises' with such violence that eventually my father, teary-eyed and gasping like a Wilfred Owen poem, would ask in a strangulated falsetto whether anyone wanted to go to the toilet?

To this day, to this minute, immediately after someone asks a question with a blindingly obvious answer, I'll hear a voice across 50 years asking in a Cork accent, made even more high pitched by the stress of trying to maintain consciousness in a fart-fog so dense you could sew a button on it, whether anyone wants to go to the toilet?

These homespun scenes only occurred if there wasn't a match on. If there was a match on, then 10 concentrated gobbling minutes after the gravy-whisking stopped, himself, Gunga and myself were in the car and on our way to a match. This being Limerick that meant a rugby match, and my father being from Cork that meant Garryowen.

Under the influence of some commercial reps he was in digs with in Cork – and to his mother's republican fury – he had played Junior Cup for Cork Constitution and so was automatically disposed to Garryowen when he came to Limerick; those two and St Mary's in Dublin enjoying a recognised but casual affiliation. He was friendly, too, with the 'Skin' McCarthys who were a founding family of the club which had its origins in the city's famous pig trade. Limerick's pork butchers and pig buyers were a caste that did business together, intermarried and had very definite notions about who they were and what they represented. They were not people who suffered from a deficit of self-esteem and Garryowen RFC was the sporting expression of that. They were proud of their traditional free-flowing running style and slightly over-emphasised egalitarian principles, but in the truest traditions of the Irish their best explanation of what they were was to be garnered by fully understanding what they were not.

And what they were not was either Shannon or Young Munsters.

Shannon had originally served as a feeder club to Garryowen but then, in an unpardonable act of social and sporting presumption, they had sought and – through the machinations of mischievous Cork clubs – been granted senior status, permitting the ungrateful apprentices to set up shop in treacherous competition to their erstwhile master. They drew their support from 'The Parish' (the old Englishtown) and espoused an uncompromising 'pack' or forward-orientated game that meant that their players numbered past 10 were superfluous in any attacking sense and served exclusively to tackle opposing attackers and show how many hues of blue stationary human legs could turn of a cold February afternoon.

They had a famous singing tradition rehearsed in their unofficial clubhouse, Angela Cowhey's on Sir Harry's Mall, where Frankie Flynn or Mick Yelverton would clutch the counter to brace themselves to get up to the top notes for *Hear My Song, Violetta* or their club anthem *There Is An Isle*. Not being 'properly' from Limerick, we were immune to the worst bitterness that resulted from their rebellion against the natural order and Eamon Clancy, with whom my father did business, was a staunch man for them and a member of their first Senior Cup winning team in 1960. We just couldn't work up the preferred level of animosity towards them and my father secretly admired their absolute discipline and commitment to the coalface aspect of the game. It was impossible, however, for even us to ignore the crackling tension that ran the few miles and vast animosity between Garryowen and Young Munster.

Like the Red Branch Knights or the Templers, the origins of 'Munsters' were clouded in mystery and legend; they reputedly had been named as tribute to the British Army's local regiment, the Munster Fusiliers, and the black-and-amber, tiger-striped jerseys were a nod to that regiment's own antecedents in the private army of the East India Company. Whatever about that – and that wouldn't have been something to advertise from the late 60s onwards – they were now so completely identified with the local operation of CIE, the state transport company, that they resembled one of those officially approved football clubs from the communist bloc, Dynamo Moscow or Lokomotive Leipzig.

The membership of Lokomotive Limerick lived in the streets and corporation estates adjacent to the train station and works, and their relationship and identification with their club was total and of the 'to-the-death' variety. Their acute (and correct) suspicion that they were looked down on was turned into a magnificent reverse snobbery that had you ineligible to be admitted into their innermost sanctums if you *didn't* work in CIE or had any kind of proprietary or managerial connection with the mercantile or commercial classes.

Their players were similarly grown from within and were seldom from outside their own 'Back of the Monument' bailiwick of Carey's Road and Prospect, much less from outside Limerick. Experiments with outsiders were not particularly successful and the dismal showing at stud of a giant Boer second row they imported for an unofficial breeding programme only confirmed them in their conviction that everyone was against them, and they must rely on their own efforts. Their hyper-sensitivity and capacity to take offence was legendary and the whole club had nearly suffered a collective apoplexy when a player from one of the tiny number of Dublin clubs who would deign to play them sauntered over to an injured Munsters' man and offered the medical expertise gathered in his occupation – as a vet.

That persecution complex resulted in an obsession with the exact observation of procedure and etiquette, and an icy defiance, that was superb to behold. For Garryowen, the glamour boys, the JFK to their Nixon, was the coldest corner of a frozen heart reserved. On the days when the respective senior teams were drawn to meet, we would play each other at several age groups starting with Under-10s and increasing with age (and ferocity) till the seniors kicked off in the afternoon. The routine at their grounds in Greenfields was the same and one that issued a silent scream that they were 'As-Fucking-Good-As-Any'.

We would arrive to be met by one of their officials wearing one of the interchangeable CIE/Young Munsters black blazers and a rictus grin, his NCO's 'Stand at Ease' hands-behind-your-back stance recalling the whispers about their base, red-coated ancestors. 'Yeer welcome, lads. Yeer dressing rooms are on the right... anything yee need just ask for it. There's a bite for yee afterwards... it's only skirts and kidneys. (And then the voice coagulating with hate)... But sure yee might be hungry enough...'

Garryowen were the Cavaliers, floppy hatted fly-halves and dashing backline cavalry charges. If cuffs had to be handed out 'in the loose', then they should be of the lace variety. Young Munsters played the Roundheads, grim and unsmiling, biblical in their smiting of those who scorned the good book (the train timetable). They were contemptuous of decoration and frivolity, convinced that it was easier for a camel to get through the eye of a needle than it was to get a rich man through a backline of properly motivated and hard-tackling fitters and diesel mechanics. Regarding the successful suburbanites of Garryowen and Cork Con from the warren of engine workshops and sidings in Colbert Station they were, literally, the rugby club from the wrong side of the tracks. But they had something about them.

And you just had to concede they had something about them. They gave off sparks. There was the perpetual underdog's stoicism; if they met triumph or disaster on the pitch they treated both imposters the same and, unsurprisingly, they had a shop steward's obsession with procedural minutiae that only made any lapses – like the occasion they heaved their goat mascot off Sarsfield Bridge and into the river on their way back into town from Thomond Park after a cup final defeat – more spectacular and endearing.

They had a dark charisma that nibbled away at ancient familial loyalties. Richard Harris' public defection to Young Munster was the Philby moment; he had played for Garryowen and through his school would have been welcomed at Old Crescent. But he looked past the clubs that would have expected his allegiance as their right and chose instead their smouldering resentful rival. Lear looked past Edgar and Cordelia, and chose Edmund.

Limerick had five senior clubs; in addition to the Big Three, there was Bohemians RFC, a light-punching, dilettante outfit comprising bank and insurance officials, whose anthem *When The Red, Red Robin Comes-a Hop, Hop, Hopin' Along* sent all the wrong signals about the level of resistances required to beat serious Garryowen, Cork Con or Shannon outfits. Old Crescent was the standard 'old boys' club for Crescent College, the school that sons of the city's Catholic bourgeoise attended. They too were drawn from the legal and financial communities, but they had a Jesuit-instilled depth and a confidence about who they were that the more unsure Bohs never transmitted. This quiet poise was remarkable for the fact that it was maintained even in their clubhouse, a damp, windowless, concrete, Fuhrer bunker up between the sprawling council estates of Rathbane and Southill where cars were conspicuously rare and where ex-classmates of Harris watching Crescent against Dolphin and startled by a sudden whinny, could wheel around on the touchline and find themselves looking at a sizable war band of hard-eyed and be-denimed young braves, sprawling bareback on their piebald mounts, twisted rope bridles looped around dot-tattooed knuckles. Watching knowledgably and applauding politely a nerveless catch-and-mark by a full back before a murmured order had them turn and canter off to resume their original mission. Every bit as unknowable and unsettling as the Indians Dickie himself had to keep hiding from in *Man in the Wilderness* when that had been shown in the Lyric or Royal or Savoy or Carlton or one of the other Limerick cinemas.

We regularly went to Cork for matches, the Mardyke, Musgrave Park or out to 'Con' at Temple Hill, but it was a bit of a haul up and down in winter, especially for a man who was on the road every other day of the week. So if Garryowen were down in Cork, it usually meant an afternoon of farty operetta unless 'Con' were up in Limerick in which case we could fly out to Thomond Park and try and catch Beecher Lynch or any of the other lads my father knew from his stint with them. On the sensible basis of seeing everyone while they were at it, the Cork lads would look into Myles Breen's for a couple of pints before they headed down home.

That famous bar was a DMZ but with closely monitored casual 'spheres of influence' within: Bohs in front (the only place they ever were, said the wags) and Garryowen and some Shannon in the middle and back. Pint after pint of Guinness was filled and handed out, while Gunga and myself sat in a corner under strict instructions to decline politely any offers of Taytos and lemonade. If someone persisted to a third offer my father would give a micro-nod and we could accept.

Eyeing the clock on the television, we would frantically stuff them into our mouths before The Angelus began because the sudden silence that began with the first mournful 'DONG' hugely amplified the crunching from the Taytos and drew disapproving glances from others and a petrifying black stare from himself. The silence continued for the news and the identification of whoever had been shot or blown up that day in the North, and the quiet was turned up to deafening for that day's sports results which were given in order of respectability: GAA, then horse racing, then rugby, golf, athletics, then slowing down to show-jumping, another touch on the brakes for that day's car racing from Mondello, perhaps a little aside about the weekend's hare coursing or hockey, an earnest bright delivery to try and unsuccessfully disguise the irrelevance of whatever it was they'd got up to that day in the country's only indoor gym at Belfield, before the League of Ireland's soccer results scraped the bottom of the sporting and social-respectability barrel.

The tension around announcement of the club rugby results was stoked by the inordinate length of time it took the announcer to work through the day's various gaelic football and hurling results, with every individual fixture having to be prefaced and contextualised by the association's eye-glazing complex league structure.

'Hurling. Division B Two North. Second Round. Fermanagh, three points... London, a goal and one point.'

By now, half the men in the country were well into their mid-teens of pints consumed and the teatime drives home were slow and deliberate. Like the legendary donkeys that had safely conveyed their unconscious forefathers home from the pub or fairs for centuries gone by, the Hillmans, Vauxhalls and Fords waited patiently outside for their drink-sodden masters to climb in before self-activating a primitive homing device that – functioning on the electromagnetic principle of like charges repelling – enabled the many hundreds of drunk drivers to avoid each other as they slowly criss-crossed the city wending their white-knuckled, rheumy-eyed way homewards.

After he dropped Gunga and myself home for our tea, my father would immediately turn the car around and head down to 'The Hurlers' for his last five pints; he was on the clock now because he had to be back in time for *The Riordans*, the nation's must-see television show dealing with the lives and loves of the eponymous farm family and set in fictional village of Leestown. The show contained classic 'Seventies-will-be-socialist' beard-stroking questioning of traditional mores, and clunking introductions of advanced agronomics and the most modern farming practices, thus: 'The whole herd is destroyed with Rectal Splat and the scutters. Is this brown bread, mam, or do I need to wash me hands?'

National attention focused on the efforts of the family's son and heir, Benji a Macra na Feirme version of Bobby Ewing, to get a shift, or 'a feel', or receive any kind of sexual relief at all from his girl, Maggie.

Poor Benji's slurry-speckled and increasingly desperate attempts, as he approached his forties, to blow a load backed up since Vatican II only aroused a level of metropolitan derision that had any country boys (culchies) who asked Dublin girls for a dance being sneeringly dismissed as 'having the smell of Benji' about them.

Interestingly, according to the internet's 'Urban Dictionary', contemporary usage of 'the smell of Benji' refers to an aroma perceived to emanate from a dog's ejaculation.

Wouldn't you like to be explaining that to Minnie Brennan?

The show's end credits rolled down the screen with the characters still clearly visible behind, soundlessly carrying out their workaday farming activities, waving sticks at each other in greeting, rubbing poteen liniment into greyhounds or stuffing kittens into a hessian sack and heading off purposefully to the riverbank, all to the jaunty orchestral reworking of *The Palatine's Daughter* that was the theme music and alternative national anthem.

As the last notes ended, Ireland's thoughts ruefully turned to whatever obstacles and drudgery the week ahead held. Because it didn't matter what the clock said, Monday began as soon as *The Riordans* ended, and so we sat savouring every last second of Sunday before the nation stood wearily, gave a whole-body yawn that, at the very limit of the stretch, loudly expelled the last pockets of trapped intestinal gases caused by the day's vast consumption of boiled vegetable and potato pandy. This was the national klaxon that announced the sabbath was nearly finished and we should begin putting our Sunday shoes, Sunday clothes, Sunday records, Sunday hair, Sunday sibling truces, Sunday acoustics – where the occasional passing car or faraway dog bark achieved recording studio clarity in the afternoon stillness, a Dolby *Dé Domhnaigh* – into the mental tallboy where, placed and folded carefully, they would sit for the week, to be brought out and reassumed seven days later.

6

Gandhi Never Ate a Raisin

IF DRIVING AROUND was recreational, then it was 'a spin', but if business-related it automatically became 'a run'. Seani's business itinerary was semi-fixed and so took a definite article... it was 'The Run'.

Technically, the run began at Clancy's store at the junction of Ellen Street, Michael Street and Mungret Street, across from the Watergate Flats, where Mike Flanagan, one of the lads in the store lived. If we were running behind and every minute counted, then Gunga and myself would go in to help load the truck. But working on his usual basis that you should never do what a commercial transaction obliged the other party to do ("There's no point keeping a dog and barking yourself"), Seani would read his *Irish Press* up in De Vito's Continental Cafe, checking the day's listings of Ireland's twin obsessions: deaths and horse racing ('hearses and horses') and call into Saint Michael's to say a prayer on the way back to their store by which time the Clancys would have loaded his truck the way he wanted.

He would then drive out to meet us, our boyish reserves of strength undiminished, at the Castletroy lights on the main Dublin Road out of Limerick.

We climbed on board there and then trundled slowly out to Birdhill, through the village itself before turning left and northwards, down the straight road towards the bridge across the Shannon at Ballina… to Killaloe and Clare beyond. As the road approached the river, it veered into a right-angled turn that had it run parallel to the Shannon for the last mile into Ballina. On a sunny day the gaps in the tunnel of high roadside trees and the white light bouncing off the river just the other side combined for an epilepsy-inducing strobe effect in the truck cab. If the flicker was fast enough to work up a momentary disco slow-mo effect then Gunga would sit up straight, do the Travolta diagonal hip-to-sky point and break into a pitch-perfect Bee Gees warble falsetto.

What we doin' out of bed and in the back, ah
what we doin out of bed and lifting sacks, ah
Should be relaxing, yeah, relaxing, yeah

He might still be singing it when we emerged from the tree tunnel into the full Studio 54 glory of the eye-blinding, mile-wide, sparkling mirror ball of Lough Derg and our first stop at Ballina.

Loading the truck was not the humdrum task that the phrase implies. This was pre-pallet and pre-health and safety. Everything, from a ton of potatoes down to a punnet of strawberries, went on by hand and the resultant balancing act challenged every law of physics.

Apples went top left. Oranges mid-to-bottom left. Bananas top right. Tomatoes mid-to-bottom left.

The hard cannonball-like Dutch cabbages went bottom left with dozens of net-bagged turnips and parsnips. The whole rear of the truck was a sandbag wall of potatoes, a solid block comprising interlocked and supporting layers of four-stone bags. There could be 80 or more. On top of these wobbling columns of boxed apples, bananas, potatoes and oranges were placed trays and shallow boxes of peaches, grapes, gooseberries, shallots and – on foot of repeated entreaties by the Dutch and German hippies who lived in the hills behind Tulla and Mountshannon – red, green and yellow peppers, which we tapped upon and held up to our ear, listening for a response, like lonely prisoners in adjoining cells, surreptitiously turning them around in our hands looking for the perforations, too embarrassed to ask each other how Saxa got the white spicy dust out.

The best way to imagine our outward journey fully laden is to consider the boxes and more regular bags as tectonic plates with the gaps between them, on which we would place trays of punnet strawberries, as the fault lines. The idea was that the more fixed columns would wobble away against each other but the carefully plotted 'give' would always ensure that balance was maintained by a counter-wobble.

The grapes, gooseberries and the other fancies skimmed above the shifting masses elevated from any danger of crushing or pulping, able to breath and providing a rewardingly exotic vista for any of presumptuous shopkeepers who might want to 'have a look in the back'.

The Dutch cabbages – the stacker's despair – were the San Andreas Fault of this arrangement. They were the hard, white, bland, cabbages that had invaded the country and were systematically clogging the greener and more pungent York variety off the shelves and into historical cookbooks. The Dutch cabbages were impossible to lay down in any state of order and, despite stacking them with neurosurgical sensitivity, nothing could be balanced on them and even within their net bags they turned like ball-bearings.

The very first serious corner we took (the right-hand veer into the strobe tunnel) was instantly followed by a massive lurch that announced that the Dutch had gone over the tomatoes and into the little Viet Cong tunnel, through the pile of stuff that was the extraction route that Gunga and I were expected to use.

The summer run was more lucrative than its winter counterparts and that extra margin was largely derived from the makings of salads. We sold huge amounts of lettuce purchased from Clancy's, who in turn bought it off Lynch's, and quite possibly this lettuce was the only ingredient of the Irish summer salad of that era that a foreigner would even recognise as a foodstuff.

The Irish 70s salad was a descendent and derivative of the legendary national 'cold tay' in the same way that we might say that AIDS is a derivative of some unspeakable sexually transmitted monkey 'clap'. We had only the vaguest idea of what it is we were trying to achieve and really were dependent on what the English thought was the way to go. The results were predictably awful, and the Irish salad of the 60s and 70s should be considered as the last stand of pre-Vatican II Ireland in the culinary sense.

In the same way as RTÉ presenters and panels aped their BBC and ITV counterparts by smoking pipes and wearing suede jackets, our own salads aped what the mammy had seen the sister in Hammersmith serving. Alongside the bottled deep purple beetroot and green-hued half-boiled egg, there also sat a somewhat vague fear that the bluff might be called; that someday, someone, who actually knew what went into a salad, might pull up a chair and wonder aloud what the fuck this was meant to be?

The principal ingredient of the original cold tay was roughly square slices of processed meat. This could be either corned beef or ham (always pronounced as 'homm' in Seani's home county of Cork) and no-one would turn a hair if they were given slices of spam with the great globules of transparent fat and gristle all surrounded with a delicate offal-flavoured trim. The corned beef too was speckled with medium sized panes of transparent fat, through which we would look at each other and poke out with our tongues till told to restore it to our plate, think of the children in Africa and eat it up.

The king of the plate was the ham, and every shop worthy of the name had a slicer festooned with bits of old cuts and slices in various stages of curliness the way an old soldier wore his ribbons. You could easily imagine that the ham came from a real animal in a way that, for instance, would be impossible where the corned beef was concerned.

The cold tay bequeathed these meats to the Irish salads along with other priceless heirlooms like a half a tomato and a half a boiled egg. And these provided the backdrop against which some questionable impressionistic strokes were added.

A slice of cucumber, a cold onion ring… a boiled and cooled potato cut into cubes and individually coated with Heinz Salad Cream… a scallion, an occasional scoop of pickle ('peeeekle').

Directly opposite the meat to signify a status only slightly less, a thumb would gently dislodge a lump of Heinz Vegetable Salad from the serving teaspoon to fall into position. The vegetable salad had the consistency of cold vomit and something also of its taste, as I was to discover a couple of years later when I began drinking my own experimental cocktails. It had a vaguely gastric smell and I seem to recall its chief ingredients as being chopped carrots and peas. I can't be sure. These are repressed memories, and the secrets of vegetable salad are revealing themselves one retch at a time.

The Rule of Thumb (the same one used to dislodge the 57 varieties of vomit) was straightforward: Without lettuce and vegetable salad, it's a cold tay. With both of these ingredients, it's a salad and – if we consider the composition of the meat – it's a salad with knobs on. Pigs' knobs.

After leaving our first stop, we would drive up the Garrykennedy Road out of Ballina and perform a 17-point turn where the road widened and branched off for the primary school. We then headed back down the way we'd just come and back into the heart of the village, where we would turn right and over the bridge that spanned the Shannon and carried you over to Killaloe and the hills of East Clare that lay north and west of that little town.

The bridge was narrow and an unspoken etiquette dictated that trucks or 'lurries' had the right of way, with cars expected to pull over at either end of the bridge till the wider commercial vehicles were over and so avoid those embarrassing paint-scraping encounters in the middle where fixed smiles and muttered obscenities were exchanged. The locals generally observed the rule, the 'heepies' – Dutch and German people who lived in the rural hinterland, wore clogs, made cheese and to general hilarity talked about protecting nature – also were scrupulous in their adherence to local mores. The problem would come with the arrival of the summer tourist cars and it most specifically occurred where yellow-plated British or Northern Irish cars would dreadnought their way onto the bridge and then calmly inch their way past us while Seani sent a volley of abuse their way, and from our elevated position in the cab of the truck drew our attention to the tartan picnic blanket visible in the British car.

What good were picnics to the Irish economy? Why couldn't they stop somewhere and have a bite to eat sitting up at a table like decent people, instead of climbing over gates, showing their varicose veins and startling heifers so that they could throw down their tartan blankets on the wet grass to eat their own sandwiches and drink tea out of their matching tartan flasks.

How did Ireland benefit from that, he would ask.

Did they even know how their so-called soldiers had shot men dead on this same bridge not so long ago? Four local men had been shot down like dogs against the parapet of this bridge. Indeed, they were. And too easily forgotten now by some who should remember. Did we know the Rodgers in Scariff? One of them was murdered by the British in 1920 on this very bridge and here they were now, in their Austin fucking Allegro, holding up working men and creating chaos on the same bridge nearly 60 years later.

They'll never change. *Never.*

Seani's dad, Dan MacCarthy had gone on a 30-odd day hunger strike in Cork jail while imprisoned there during the Troubles. His mother, who he insisted (paging Dr Freud!) that we too referred to as 'mother' had also been imprisoned in Cork and Kilmainham jails courtesy of the British and the Free State. We were, in the parlance of the time, 'Black Fianna Fail' where that signified loyalty to the most fervent school of constitutional Republicanism and an aversion to the most demeaning and insidious trappings of our erstwhile masters.

We'd be talking there about tweed suits, pipe-smoking, suede, recreational gardening ('Wasn't it well for them? The Irish had to dig for a *living*!'), jam-making, moleskin or twill trousers, Elgar, beer or ale, tins of shortbread decorated with Highland scenes, kippers, embroidery or needlepoint, kindness to animals.

We'd also be talking about certain types of hard-boiled sweets (anything too redolent of urchins looking through mullioned windows or similar early period Victoriana) and anything or anybody that proclaimed itself 'By Appointment to…'.

Also to be regarded warily were men's polo necks, fly fishing, ivy, maintained woodland, pedigree cattle breeding, ponds – especially ponds containing ducks that paddled in Royal Navy line-ahead Spithead review formation – meat pies, hunting from horseback, moustaches, pork (bacon that had taken the soup), Brown Windsor (soup that had taken the soup), driving gloves, blazers (especially striped 'Henley' ones), titles other than papal, topiary, lawn ornaments, seated band recitals, craft cheese, a passion for motorbikes or vintage cars, botany, croquet, overly-fussy car cleaning, cravats, singing in church, garden herbs, umbrella-twirling (or any other form of City of London umbrella affectation), taxidermy, marmalade (Could you get more Orange? The UVF in jam form), allotments, woollen ties and slippers.

The issue of preserves and pickles was complicated but important: homemade chutney smacked of Protestant frugality and could be frowned upon, while shop bought was acceptable – excepting Sherwood's which, with its Raj origins and 'Robin of….' English folk hero echo – was suspect. Branston's Ploughman's Pickle, with its nod towards wind-whipped cheeks and a miserable trudge through knee-high shit behind a pair of harmoniously flatulent horses at least conjured up the vision of doing some physical work yourself and so was the Republican relish-of-choice.

The colour-coded domestic political spectrum referred to was a somewhat counter-intuitive affair. Thus 'Black Fianna Fail' actually meant 'Green Non-Provo', while 'Black Fine Gael' could mean 'Home Rule Green Redmonite farmers who like riding to the hounds'. The more aggressive 'street' variant of 'Black Fine Gael' could be described, by reference to history, as 'Black Blue Shirts'.

Ultra-loyalists from the 'Black North' were dismissed as 'Black Orange', while the astonishing news that there were Orange lodges in Ghana meant that we had to add a new category… 'Black Orange Black'. The emergence of the environmental movement at the end of the 70s and their adoption of the sobriquet 'Green' marked the end of any coherence in attempts to categorise people on the National Question by reference to colour.

The dual meanings of 'Green' now meant that under the old classification a diehard 'Just Society' Fine Gaeler with a growing interest in the environment had to be rendered as a 'Pinko Green Black Blueshirt'. Not even the Irish, the most politically nuanced people in the galaxy, were able to follow it much further than this without carrying round paint shop colour charts for reference, and so the political pigmentation shorthand is now used very infrequently and that inexpertly.

Our dad, Seani, came from Macroom, a town in mid-Cork that was justly proud of the ferocious reputation it had gained during the 1919-21 struggle against the Tans. Whenever he mentioned to people that he was from Macroom, they would immediately come back with the traditional rejoinder, 'The town that never reared a fool', an anonymous and popular testament to the town's legendary capacity for producing shrewd operators. Whatever about that and amongst his Limerick-born children, Macroom was referred to as 'The town that never turned on an oven' because none of us had ever eaten a hot bite within 10 miles of the town's landmark, its castle, which Seani's mother had enthusiastically helped to burn down when the Tans withdrew from it in 1921. In the same way as Nice could be said to have perfected the concept of the European Summer salad, our Macroom relations had distilled the 'cold tay' down to its very heart-breaking essence.

Nowhere else was the lettuce limper; nowhere else had gristlier corned beef; no-one else's eggs were greener; nowhere else had 'homm' with the slightly fizzy fluorescent aftertaste that denoted mere minutes to go before it was unfit for human consumption. At the table of our Macroom relations, you were eating against the clock.

On the three or four occasions during the year when they did decide to actually cook food only one method of preparation seemed acceptable. Whether it was sprats (baby herrings), wild mushrooms, mutton or crubeens, a slow simmering in milk for three or four hours was deemed your only man. Till the day he died, my father thought it the only method of cooking worthy of effort, and drool would thicken his tongue till the words became guttural yelps and yips as he described the childhood arrival of the sprat truck in the town where it would be besieged and rocked from side to side as hysterical Macrumpians began waving money at the driver, while trying to remember where they had left their skillets and pots after last year's usage.

'The truck... sprats... park up in the town square. I'd to find a kettle to carry the feeesh... mother, auntie Kate... run down... fight to buy them... then bring them back up to Danzig to auntie Kate's. Boiled in milk for two hours...you never tasted anything like it. Then drink the milk. Stop it. Eat your own fingers.'

Whenever the subject of food was raised or touched upon – and provided my mother wasn't present – he'd go through a list of dishes and delicacies that could only be done justice by a quick five-hour lactose simmering or overnight marinade in milk. He'd start simmering away himself and eventually come to the boil with Tourette-style imprecations and complaints about the way milk had been patronised and disdained as a cooking ingredient by unnamed social climbers (herself) and other followers of the recipes contained in 'that Orange bastard Beaverbrook's Fleet Street rags'.

'Kid goat.... I'll have it again... by God, I will... in my house... in milk... I don't like it braised and I don't want braised... those BASTARDS... the whole country ate mushrooms in milk."

Nor did the milk of his kindness extend to her recipe for curry. The concept itself wasn't a problem, his objection rested on a gratuitous addition that he suspected had been decided upon in Dublin and not Delhi, and most likely at the suggestion of his bête noire via the Woman's page in his *Daily Express*.

'Jesus Christ, who puts raisins in their dinner? The Indians don't put raisins in curry but ye know better in Clonskeagh... the Indians don't! But ye'll do what that Canadian bastard tells ye to do... ye always did... what do the Indians know about curry? Shure they only invented it! Gandhi never ate a raisin in his life! But ye know better in Dublin.'

In Macroom, we'd generally park down in Danzig (real name, Barrett's Place), a small council estate completed (I assume) just before the war and precipitating intense negotiations, uneasy co-existence and peace brokering around the allocation of the three-dozen odd houses that earned it the nickname. I never heard Seani refer to it as anything else.

His Aunty Kate, whose fish-flavoured boiled milk still enslaved his palate 40 years later, lived there. Her other speciality was a terse sounding rabbit stew ('catch it, gut it, skin it, boil it in milk'). Like her sister, Hannah, Seani's mother, she too had been thrown in jail by the

British and the Free State. The girls were industrious and spirited and very, very serious about their cause. They were hard on backsliders and traitors in that way that convinced Cork women can be. But they seemed to have a bit about them as well. They liked a laugh; they liked a little nip in the evening when their long day's work was done, and they loved their clothes. They had tailored snappy little overcoats out of prison issue blankets for their release.

Hannah, 'Mother', was the senior partner.

She ran the business, and she was tough. She'd a couple of businesses and if drunken farmers kicked-up in one of her places on a Fair Day, then she bounced them out herself. She didn't give her kids holiday money; she gave them stuff to sell to raise their holiday money. She didn't take holidays herself. Ever. And she pulled dad out of school at 13 or 14 to drive her around as she attempted to keep her little business empire on the road. He told me that he was once stopped wearing short pants by the Guards while driving her around.

Her husband, Seani's dad, Dan, shot himself in 1938.

If we asked, we were told it was a hunting accident. But Dan had been around guns and knew how to use them. One day we were on 'The Run' and parked up on the banks of Lough Derg having a bite to eat when a man came over to the open truck window to ask the name of the hills opposite on the Tipperary side. He had a superb Cork accent with sudden rises and abrupt falls like a fast blindfolded stroll over an irregularly ploughed field, and Seani eventually gave in and asked him whereabouts in Cork he was from? He was from a small place called Carriginima, near the town of Macroom. Why? Did Seani know people there?

Seani said that he was from that very town. He was one of the MacCarthys on the Main Street. The man immediately asked whether he was anything to the 'IRA man, Dan MacCarthy'. Seani said he was his son and the man waited just a few silent seconds before drifting away in what was by the standards of Irish country people a very abrupt and offensive manner. The 'who-do-you-know-that-I-might-know' fencing had ended immediately upon the connection with Dan who, it was patent, had done something that the man felt was beyond even the mildest of discussion that should have come naturally after the passing of 40-odd years.

I never asked Seani right out what he thought had happened because the (maybe) eight times the subject came up his voice took on a very unfamiliar faraway tone and he would start explaining, as if to a coroner, about how the trigger on the reversed shotgun had snagged on a bramble going through the ditch after the hunting dogs. He was only six when it happened and I think a little bit of that day's hopelessness and despair got into him, pulled up a chair in some corner, and sat down, silently trying to catch his eye for the rest of his life. I only remember him ever once volunteering a mention of his father.

Years later, he asked me did I want to go for a pint one night and when we were sitting down in O'Shea's, he very quietly said that he would have loved to have gone for a drink with his father.

After calling to Strich's, the last stop in Killaloe, we would head off up west side of Lough Derg, up and over Ogonnelloe where the road overlooked the ancient home of Brian Boru, the Dalcassian king (and, incidentally, mortal foe of the Eoghanocht dynasty of which the MacCarthys were the business end). The road climbed up to a vantage point that sat with Sliabh Bernagh behind and the whole lake before you, with Clare on the left and Tipperary on the right.

Seani would note the magnificence of the view and how much it reminded him of Killarney. He would happily acknowledge that 'they say' that Donegal was beautiful. or 'I'm told' that parts of Mayo were striking. But they were necessarily flawed imitations of the Platonic ideal of natural beauty which was Killarney. Breathtaking film footage of the Yukon or Alaska shot from aeroplanes reminded him of Moll's Gap and when he questioned me about a visit to Sweden and Finland, he listened intently to my description before summing it up as 'a whole country of Muckross'.

Mostly we drove in a comfortable silence punctuated by Seani's requests to be reminded of such-and-such when we got to so-and-so's. But what diversions we got always came courtesy of my younger brother, Eoin, who I called Gunga for reasons that are now lost in time but which I seem to recall as involving him swearing pain on someone nicknamed Gunga who had attracted his displeasure.

It was easy to attract my brother's displeasure.

His character was fully formed very young, and it revealed itself in heart-warming displays of kindness towards animals and injured birds, neatly counterpointed by a propensity to accept any slight – deliberate or inadvertent – as a challenge to be met by handing out 'digs' on the jaw that were disproportionately fierce for someone of his size and reach. I'd say on his best day ever, Gunga wasn't five-foot-eight, but he had a dig like an iron bar and at age nine, and a foot smaller, he lifted me off the ground and put me on my back with a left cross punch that came up and into my nose like a little bolt of lightning.

We had the old pre-Christian faith in the spiritual properties of water in our house and most domestic scraps and cuts – from diarrhoea to dandruff – were remedied by a form of proto-waterboarding that would have raised an eyebrow in Abu Gharib 35 years later. I still had the right-hand boxing glove on (I'd given him the 'weaker' left for our spar) as I climbed gingerly into the old peeling bath and contorted myself to position my busted nose directly underneath the healing spout. The cold tap was then turned-on full bore and aimed directly down the injured nostril till the sheer volume of water and hypothermic shock stunned my nose into ceasing to bleed.

If I forgot exactly what had provoked his decision to cut loose I never,

ever, forgot the compressed force and speed and I made a mental note – even at those tender years and one which I acted on all his beautiful life – to move well back out of swinging range if I ever saw his brow begin to corrugate and his Hockney swimming pool blue eyes take on a sudden steely sheen.

Gunga read by proxy. He watched me read and then interrogated me. He was insatiably curious and very decisive about what he liked and what he didn't. When he liked, he loved. But if the object of his affections ever lapsed, or showed themselves unworthy of his affections, then they were dropped. And dropped without ado.

He had followed me reluctantly into the barely understood netherworld of heavy rock and metal bands and looked very sceptical when I contrasted the properly masculine look of Judas Priest's Rob Halford (leather chaps, black mirror shades and chain-draped leather hat) with the hopelessly fey image of obvious 'steamers' like his own favourites Lindsey Buckingham or Mick Fleetwood.

Gunga thought elliptically and intuited things on a basis both absolutely illogical but somehow indisputable. When I pointed at Rob Halford's studded codpiece on the front of Unleashed in the East and observed that this was definitely the look that girls went for and Rob probably had to beat the birds off with a shitty stick, he seemed to know, on some level, that I was getting this completely (and literally) arse-over-tit and that, actually, wearing leather underwear and mirror shades was not necessarily a reliable indicator of a healthy interest in girls. He sensed it, where I was comfortably oblivious.

My favourite song was a thunderous number by The Scorpions, a German rock band, entitled *Speedy's Coming* that I decided was a driving twin-lead guitar tribute to the Looney Tunes Mexican mouse but which, upon mature reflection, is probably a complaint about premature ejaculation. At my insistence, Gunga would sit staring at the sleeve cover of their *Tokyo Tapes* double-live album that showed a Gibson Flying V-wielding Ulrich Roth bent over so far backwards that his superbly conditioned mane brushed the Tokyo Sun Plaza stage floor. He noted the face contorted in a sonic ecstasy. He liked the back cover that featured the dwarfish singer, Klaus Meine, doing a little hop in vertiginous platform boots silhouetted against Hermann Rarebell's mandatory double bass drum kit. All this was very good and Gunga was suitably impressed. He agreed that this is what a band should look like. He acknowledged that these lads seemed to know what it was all about. But he held something back.

He was a man who liked to take things in at his own pace and give hugely important images the intense study they warranted. After whole days spent poring over the front and back sleeve photos and slowly twirling a Bill Hailey curl at the front of his head, he carefully removed the plastic cover and opened the album cover.

An archaeologist climbing into a newly discovered tomb in the Valley of the Kings couldn't have been as careful.

His eyes immediately fell upon a photo that showed Hermann, Ulrich, Klaus, Rudolph and Francis teetering across some pedestrian crossing in the Ginza in some ponderous, Krauty parody of the Abbey Road shot. The band members towered over the surrounding Tokyo office workers, not one of whom seemed the least bit bothered by the geisha girls-of-Valhalla get-up that the Germans were rocking. Gunga wasn't as unruffled or inscrutable; his jaw slowly opened and then kept going downwards in the double-hinged way jaws do when someone is genuinely shocked. His eyes bulged like a toad as he took in the skin-tight spandex leggings, the nipped-waist leather bolero jackets twinned with printed wrap-over kimonos.

Very, very slowly, almost imperceptibly, he stopped twirling his Bill Hailey kiss-curl and arced that finger down to tap very slowly and solemnly on Ulrich Roth's kitten heeled, white patent ankle boots. On the fifth tap, his whole head of hair seemed to knit together and then move a full inch backwards. After a minute or two of this stupefaction, he came to his decision and closed the sleeve. He never opened it again and reacted badly afterwards if anyone ever mentioned his previous interest in The Scorpions.

Speedy never came again.

His other chief interests at that time were ornithology and animal scatology – his collection of various species' turds and stools, both fossilised and fresh, were all kept in Chivers' jars in a drawer and carefully labelled – and the identification and surveying of likely locations for colonies of gnomes, if such creatures existed.

One Christmas Santy left a book authored by some Dutch hippies that set out the habits, customs, and dress of gnomes in a manner that suggested either an absolute knowledge of their real existence or a massive abuse of hallucinogenic materials on the part of the authors. The rest of us quickly settled on the latter. Gunga wasn't so sure. He wanted gnomes to exist. It appealed to his spiritual side. And this and his all-consuming interest in nature and topography made for exchanges in the cab of the truck, as we drove around East Clare, that must have brought our father, Seani, a man emphatically not given to wondering about the existence of gnomes, much less their residential arrangements, to the very edge of despair.

Gunga was wholly unselfconscious about his obsession and frankly didn't give a fuck who was in the cab, who we were giving a lift to or what they might think about this line of conversation – if he wanted to talk about gnomic real estate, then he bloody well would.

I wasn't so secure and lived in dread that he'd ask me in front of strangers or hitchhikers what I'd thought of, say, Bodyke as a location for any gnomes interested in getting through a hard winter who wanted easy access to water but minimal risk of flooding.

The nightmare scenario had us giving a lift to one of the pretty Butler girls from Scariff out the Mountshannon road to their farm, and my throat gradually drying as our man began to closely scan the adjacent fields or hills through the windscreen with the kind of concentration that nearly always presaged a question directed squarely at me, demanding to know what I thought of that little wood over there as a likely site for gnomes.

In fairness to Seani, he never said a word and he'd never turn to stare at us, but the cigarette at the corner of his mouth would dip diagonally as his jaw loosened its grip. The fag angle functioned as a railway signal of his concern, his distress that his two sons and heirs were off again – please Jesus no! – arguing about where the smart gnome would settle in Clare. I think as well that, as in most things, there was a patriotic element to his discomfiture: if we had to argue about where the Little People should live, could they not at least be Irish? What was wrong with our own leprechauns? Why had they to be gnomes? Middle England's favourite pixies, sitting on their manicured lawns, on that bastard Beaverbrook's Daily Express-approved red-and-white speckled toadstools, with their little fishing rods and their thatched roof wishing wells. All beers and cheers and laughing it up! (At Paddy, probably.) After being challenged about where I would build if I was a gnome, I'd wait the shortest period consistent with due consideration and then suggest a location, perhaps somewhere between Bodyke and O'Callaghan's Mills, around Biddy Blacksticks there, back near the lake.

Or I might suggest somewhere off the flat scrubby road between Kilkishin and Quinn where the tinkers camped. What about the fields between Jimmy Farrell's in Kilmurry and Knappogue Castle? To the left of that road?

Or I might bank upwards and soar back across the broad estuary into County Limerick and the Shanid heartland of the fierce Geraldines, and nominate Carrigkerry or Ballygiltenane high up on the boggy plateau between the Barna Gap and the Shannon. Maybe I'd suggest that lovely hilly ground around the ruined Desmond castle at Ballyhahill, half-way between Glin and Rathkeale, where once the Earl composed Gaelic verse and disposed of his private army of 16,000.

Or I could have suggested the roof garden of the best hotel in Knightsbridge. Or the miniature golf course behind the Golden Nugget casino in Las Vegas. Or anywhere really. Because the response was always the same.

'That...THAT...that's the worst place for any gnome to even think about living in. What kind of a gnome is going to live there? That's the worst possible place you could have picked. You're not thinking about this. What about stoats? Where's your cover from the stoats? Or owls.

'That place is alive with owls. You wouldn't have a night's peace in that house. How would the gnomes go outside for a couple of twigs for the fire? Your problem is...you don't know enough about nature to pick the kind of place that's suitable for gnomes. And what's worse (a sad little shake of the head) is that I don't know if you're even bothered about learning. That's what's most depressing... you don't know, and you don't care that you don't know.'

Our rather strained convention dictated that I accept the reproach and gratefully note the more-in-sorrow-than-anger tone in which it had been reluctantly delivered. On most other stuff, he asked and I answered.

On any questions pertaining to gnomes and specifically what they wanted in terms of dormouse stabling and communal living, then the roles reversed. If we went out there today and he nodded up towards some hill or copse in our old signal for me to make the argument for it as a possible location for a gnome hamlet, I'd be stunned if he didn't listen in silence, wearing an intense expression, before shooting my survey to shit on grounds of vulnerability to badgers or the dangers presented by falling conkers. Yes. Falling conkers.

Surely I noticed the tree towering over the site I was recommending? Please Jesus just confirm that I could identify it as a Horse chestnut. Did

I know or did I care that the smallest conker in that tree falling from that height would crush any gnome's skull like a bowling ball dropped on an egg?

'Shure, think about it: proportionally that tree is the same to the gnomes as the Empire State building is to us. What chances would you give yourself if every autumn you had to live under the Empire State... with bowling balls dropping off it by the minute, and whistling down while you tried to go about your business?

'Would you fancy your chances in a little bothy or tigeen made of twigs and turf bonded together with finches' spittle in those circumstances? But you're perfectly happy to let the gnomes exist like that and still call yourself a decent man?'

A long sigh and a look out the window... and then.

'You don't know enough about nature to pick the kind of place that's suitable for gnomes. And even after all these years when you had a chance to learn – when you could have learned if you'd been bothered – you still don't know.

'That's what's most depressing... you don't know, and you don't care that you don't know.'

7

(I Don't Have A) Timber Heart

THERE WAS A lot of pulling and mullocking on the Clare Run, and a savage amount of criss-crossing the east of the county where you might have to double-back to sell some more stuff into an early call if someone further on in 'The Run' didn't need as much as you'd held for them.

It was a long day for young lads and a hungry one, because we usually didn't stop to eat. The only fast food available was the soup served in a few pubs and that was a choice of two, Red or Brown. Anywhere else in the Europe of those times, asking someone whether they were 'Red' or 'Brown' was to ask them whether they supported the inevitable triumph of the proletariat or whether they espoused the national socialism of Hitler's SA brown-shirted goons. Were they Left or Right?

In Ireland, the question would be heard as asking whether you preferred powdered tomato or powdered oxtail soups. I suppose a third choice could have been arrived at by blending the red and brown, but for obvious reasons the orange hued result could not be entertained.

Our 'To Go' option was a Swiss roll torn into hunks or a packet of jam tarts washed down with a pint of milk. But even this was not straightforward; Seani was fluent in small town semiotics and thought that working men eating shop-bought cake in the cab of a dusty truck was mixing messages dangerously and inviting the traditional observation to anyone eating a cake not baked by a female relative: 'Isn't it a great little country?' Or its even more loaded variant: 'Isn't it well for ye?' Involved, as we were, in the food business, that last one could hurt us, particularly if followed through to its sourest conclusion.

'Isn't it well for ye, with your Gateaux jam tarts – I notice yeer not atein' yeer own bananas.'

Avoiding any possibility of that denouement became something of an obsession for Seani. So we would hide behind ramparts of cellophaned toilet rolls or Tayto boxes in the stores at the rear of the shops, and hunker down to tear into the Swiss rolls and slug down our milk, exchanging anxious stares if a door was heard to open or a whistled tune or squeaky trolley wheel announced the proximity of anyone who might stumble upon the three of us and take in the incriminating scene before noting that it was, indeed, a great little country and wondering why it was that none of the kind of fruit we were after selling her daddy was good enough for ourselves.

There was the additional threat that, hidden from view, you might be a helpless witness to something so toe-curling that you had to stay hidden till the people involved had left the room and the three of us could emerge, stiff and cramped from our cardboard box bunker, saucer-eyed and reeling from what we'd heard.

One Saturday morning the three of us were tucked away inside a ziggurat made of stepped boxes of toilet rolls and completely hidden from view. We were working our way through our usual 'Elevenses': handfuls of chocolate log washed down with milk drank and dribbled direct from the pint bottles.

The shopkeeper's daughter and her pals came in, and thinking they were alone immediately began to discuss the various permutations and combinations of 'shifts' that they had been involved in at the previous night's hop. They hadn't even given us the chance to declare our presence and now – 'Mikey nearly twisted the chest off me' – it was too late: we had already heard too much.

The girls hopped up on the roof our little Andrex igloo and began hearing the evidence and testimonies for their own midday assizes version of the local – and amorously frank – classic, The Midnight Court, where the women of Ireland appeal to a fairy judge to give them more virile men.

The charges initially involved a more-or-less orthodox minor conundrum: whether their bawneen jumpers would ever return to shape after access to their chests had been gained via the long sleeves? But they moved, and very swiftly, south of the belt onto the senior pitch that Merriman, buried just north up the road in Feakle, had marked out for them 150 years previously: when were they going to find men worthy of the passion that raged within what was left of their chests after Mikey's pulling and mauling.

Seani's eyes widened, and he began to make fluttering signs of the cross that denoted the presence of something holy or horrible. He put his index finger to his lips in the universal signal for silence, then pointed at each of us in turn and mimed putting his fingers into his ears before pointing vehemently back at us.

We obeyed, but I was agog to hear and so bowed my head and stared at the ground in a way that I slyly knew he would interpret as understandable boyish embarrassment, but which allowed me to hear better. On and on they went, this lad was 'a ride' and a rival for his affections was 'only a bitch'.

They basked in their bawdiness, spreading out and lounging on the pile beneath which we cowered. The attention one boy was giving an apparently hefty girl was derided and they agreed that he needed to remember the principle that governed physical compatibility

'Wouldn't you think he'd cop-on? If you can't lift it, don't shift it!'

Seani stopped blessing himself and started pointing at his watch and miming panic. After 30-odd minutes they left, and it took us 10 minutes to find our nerve and emerge terror-stricken from our spongy little sarcophagus. When we got back into the cab of the truck, he did that fluttery blessing one last time, lit a cigarette and asked God to help Ireland.

He never thought he'd see the day or hear the like, where decent families and decent people were rearing hussies like that. Did we know who he blamed for young girls thinking, not to mind talking, like that? 'Beaverbrook?' I hesitantly nominated, the Keyser Soze of his world.

'Edna O'Brien,' he corrected, but sympathetically, to show that he liked the way I was thinking. It was all her fault that young girls would be coming out with muck like that. She should never be allowed back in the country.

Had we heard of her? (He asked this brightly with a quick sideways glance and dark expression that didn't match the tone). As it happened, I had heard of her, but with that supercharged sensitivity to change in atmosphere and tell-tale nanosecond pauses that came with being taught by Brother Hogan, I had picked up on the exaggerated carelessness with which the question had been asked.

No, we said. We'd never heard of her.

We were to keep it that way, he said grimly, the confirmation of our innocence ending the need for the charade. And, above all, we were 'on no account' to mention her name around here or further up in Tuamgraney and Scariff where she still had relations and you'd be hard put to throw a rock and not hit someone who was a cousin of hers or a former 'coort'.

'And where does she live now?' piped up Gunga.

She lived in London these days and was very, very, famous said Seani, for not entirely proper reasons, he added.

'And what does she do in London?' asked Gunga innocently

What…WHAT… does… she… DO?" repeated Seani slowly in stunned mortification. Like Debbie's dad after being told what Debbie was doing in Dallas. After a few heavy sighs and the concentrated smoking and denture-shifting that normally preceded the announcement of something he deemed important, he blurted out, 'You don't need to know what she does in London. You don't need to know what anyone is doing in London. The last man to do something useful there was Guy Fawkes!'

A minute of tense silence, before…

'And I'll tell you another who isn't helping things… Brendan Bowyer. What's his song out now… *Thank You Elvis?* Is that it? It should be… *Thank You Elvis For Making Poor Ireland As Mucky-Minded As Mississippi.*

'What do people think a Huckle-Buck is? Always remember: Aithne ciaraog, ciarog eile.'

The drive from Tuamgraney to Bodyke on a summer's evening was very beautiful. Through the trees on the left there was a chain of ancient lakes that ran up almost to the edge of the road and stretched back all dark and all-knowing towards O'Callaghan's Mills. We had only one stop back there, Biddy Blacksticks, a nine-foot high two-storey bar/shop/fishing tackle swap shop, within whose Wendy House dimensions lived the eponymous Biddy and a pack of fierce collies which, upon being told he'd a terminal sickness, her late husband had taught to guard his tiny wife.

Most days we'd go down, Seani would volunteer to test the dogs and adopt the bow-legged, two-fists-up, angry leprechaun, Notre Dame posture in which he'd then crab his way towards Biddy till the collies interposed themselves, snarling and slavering, waiting for Biddy's tone to give them their next cue.

When she spoke, their hackles would lower visibly and they'd move back to a semi-circle behind her, still looking hard and alert for any sudden movement that threatened her.

The dead husband's name was Paddy and he was the definitive authority on the local fishing. The coarse fishing in this part of Clare was, as they'd describe it themselves, 'mighty' and Biddy's played host to a very steady succession of anglers from exotic places like Wakefield and Rotherham. These lads came over every year to fish and, even beyond the sterling they brought with them, were noticeably well-liked. When the day was overcast, and the light muted – which would be nine days out of 10 – they went out early to these old lakes and fished all day for perch or pike. In the evenings, or if it was too sunny, they moved their large frames 'in't pub' and stayed inside having their drinks, smoking and chatting to the locals. Seani always stuck his head in to say hello and there'd follow a not always mutually comprehensible chat about the fishing and how they'd made their way over via the A72 and the ferry.

He always wished them good luck with it and would afterwards remark in the cab of the truck how much they must look forward to this week of relaxing and rewarding angling after 51 weeks dangling a worm in some oily sump or viscous canal. We were solemnly told to always mark the crucial distinction between these horny handed northern working men and their twill-trousered men and shrill-voiced women Home Counties equivalents for whom the hottest place in our Republican hell was to be reserved. The English, he patiently explained, worked in a perfect reversal of ourselves… the Northerners were decent men and considering the slag-heaped and chimney-dotted infernos in which their tweedy, port-quaffing, wildlife-massacring, House-of-Lords-lounging, plantation owners had them living and working, were to be considered every bit as put upon as us. They were Britannia's field slaves.

The Southern English working class, with their cardigans and obsessive-compulsive Sunday car washing, were the house slaves who wrinkled their smaller noses and stared just as disdainfully at their cotton-millin' countrymen to the North as they did at the potato-pickin' Contae

Caintes they saw when they came out on the porch to ceremonially empty the Master's chamber pot into the gardenia bush and looked Westwards at us. The Southern English could be good but, more often than not, they were not good, or as it was put, they were 'no good'.

Another tortuous, forward an inch, backwards an inch, forward an inch, 17-point turn on the narrow boreen and then back the way we had come to Bodyke and onwards to Tulla, through little lush fields and bosomy hills.

Seani didn't so much park, as simply come to a slow halt and turn the engine off, so we usually straddled the dotted line in the middle of the road. We called into Hobbins' shop and mineral bar and ritualistically admired the counter-to-ceiling pyramid display of Nash's red lemonade for the convenience of the Pioneer patrons of the next-door cinema to avail of during the intermissions. Both Mr and Mrs Hobbins wore hearing aids like little sewing machines balanced precariously on the rim of their ear, as did their adopted son, Tommy, whether out of necessity or solidarity, we never quite knew.

It made for an exhausting call as Seani burst through the door shouting out, 'GOD BLESS ALL HERE!' before conceding to the looks of blank incomprehension on their faces and going around to each individual and making a little hand-cupped tunnel from his mouth to their ears, screaming out the invocation while the veins came up on his forehead and the light came up in their eyes. Then Boyds. Then Martin Mac's.

The last took a small van up and into the remote fastnesses of East Clare and South Galway and so was a Russian nesting doll of our own operation. Sometimes we loaded individual bunches of bananas into his Transit and basked in the perfect miniature scale of his little mobile emporium: individual packets of Charms or Florida Fruits wedged into the crevices between shopping powders and impressive quantities of Milk of Magnesia, the laxative cure-all of Irish public medicine in the 70s, whose inky blue bottles were held in extra awe here within a flung black cat of the home of Biddy Early. She was a famous local witch who had once frozen an eviction party of Peelers to the road for five hours and whose future-divining blue bottle was repossessed by the Little People (Seani's leprechauns/Gunga's gnomes) in the minutes after her death.

Martin and his kids were supremely gifted traditional musicians and mainstays of the village's legendary Tulla Ceili band that was catapulted to national fame when, during the American Hostage Crisis, a contestant on RTÉ Radio's Just A Minute Quiz was asked, 'Who or what is the Ayatollah?'

And answered confidently, 'A ceili band'.

Onwards to Quin of the famous ruined abbey from whose steeple Cromwell's men had hanged the monks ("They'll never change. Never') and where the last acknowledged Chieftan of the MacNamaras, John 'Fireball', was buried in 1826. One hundred and fifty years later, when Seani, under pressure, decided to extend our house and 'put in' central heating, the builders he went to were 'Fireball' McNamaras who still displayed the bright tangerine afros that had earned the original John the nickname.

Moloneys were the people in Quin and if we hit them around early afternoon, we had to join them and their customers for 25 minutes of rapt concentration as Harbour Hotel – RTÉ Radio's coma-inducingly dull version of the BBC's already soporific The Archers – went on-air. This was another example of the 'aiming for salad but getting cold tay' syndrome already alluded to, where something the British were already doing badly was imitated and through heroic effort made worse.

John Moloney listened to it, though. And he listened to it in the most literal sense of the verb; none of your background or 'ambient' bullshit here. Everyone in the shop when it came on – and any poor fucker who entered while it was on – was expected to pick a spot to stand or sit and then give him or herself over to a session of eye-narrowed, teeth-sucking concentrated listening to a half an hour of demented domestic drama.

John himself listened with his eyes closed to eliminate the possibility of extraneous stimuli interfering with his focus.

If a mouse farted while the show was on, he immediately held up a hand to indicate that such noises-off were to cease and as the last notes of the theme music (Harvest Supper by Trevor Duncan) faded and stiff backs stretched and cramped limbs extended, he'd open his eyes and announce, with a most un-Irish smile that showed even, white, teeth, that that episode was 'only mighty', that we were all to join him in tea and a cut of bread before we went back to our business.

If I even think of it now, my back aches. All day long we stacked and dragged, pulled and lifted. Hiked the four stone sacks of potatoes in and through lino-floored labyrinths of corridors and passages where adjoining houses or tigeens had been knocked into each other for storeroom. Up and down tight spindly stairs, and in and out of stores and pantries. Under the dusty gaze of framed Padre Pios or unlit Sacred Hearts.

Always carefully putting what was going in, underneath what was already there, so it went out to the shelves in the right order. Gradually absorbing the loamy smell of potatoes into our hair and clothes and skeletally rearranging our young backs and shoulders the better to heft the sacks till, by eight or nine at night, we were more tuber than human.

The long day ended at Harry's Shop, Bar and Select Lounge between Sixmilebridge and Knappogue. Even by Irish standards the area was heaving with castles and tower houses, and being close to Shannon Airport many of these had developed a tourist offering that involved entertaining coach parties of Americans to standard Irish dinners served in shallow wooden trenchers as 'genuine medieval gruel'.

The Camelot vibe was further enhanced by the casting of local teenagers in film set surplus velvet gowns and hosiery as serving wenches and page boys.

Harry had lived in the States for years and on account of the intimate knowledge of the target market that bestowed on him, functioned as a kind of 'ganger' for the organisers of the banquets and those 'looking for a start' as a wench or a page. The costumes were kept in a dark room off the Select Lounge because the costumes faded in sunlight or, as Harry himself put it, 'daylight drains the dye out of the vilvet'. Made rigid with the sweat brought on by having to stand practically in the humongous indoor bonfires and slowly turn a pig on a spit, while being drenched by the mead spat out by the Yanks as the flat beer and cough syrup mixture provoked their gag reflex, the doublets allocated to the pages were probably harder and heavier than the suits of armour scattered around the hall.

Harry himself was 'a martyr to the shingles' and by way of response to the non-stop enquiries from regulars of the shop or pub as to how she was cuttin', would wordlessly pull up his shirt to indicate the vivid bubbled eruptions on his chest before smoothly filling their pints and skimming a plastic knife – held by his itching finger – across the creamy heads. He had been in the States for years and having decided to join the army to avail of the free dental treatment ('I'd a mouth of teeth like a witchdoctor's necklace, Sean'), he had found himself in Korea fighting the Communists, and with his straightened and filled choppers clicking with the cold 'like a tinker playing the spoons'. He claimed to be able to speak Chinese, and told us that we could travel anywhere in Asia with just that language's exclamation for surprise which he rendered as 'Hole Eee Fuk'.

He was blue in the face warning these Clare greenhorns about the Yellow Peril and the onslaught of red atheism, and he told us that any man called McCarthy could hold his head up in any bar from Hell to Hoboken because, 'God knows, "Tail-gunner Joe" was right more often than he was wrong'. He knew Asian cuisine and could tell the pedigree of the meat dishes. He confirmed Seani's suspicions that curries did not contain raisins and that it was highly unlikely that Gandhi had ever knowingly consumed a raisin – certainly not a cooked one. Mao was the same.

He drank behind the bar counter which broke The Golden Rule of Irish Publicans which was that you never took a drink from your own shelf for your own self. Like most everyone else in Clare, Harry could play the melodeon. He loved to sing, and he loved The King. After five large small ones and in response to their entreaties, he'd pick up his old 'Banner Bellows' and treat the customers to a medley that always began with the song guaranteed to have the flat-capped farmers blinking fast over moistened eyes as they remembered faithful old four-legged companions now helping to bring in the herd up in Heaven, Old Shep. Then a playful lip-curled version of *Love Me*, on to the rousing call-to-arms that was *Clare to the Front* and then, with a little nod to where the three of us sat slumped in an exhausted silence easily mistaken for speechless admiration, he'd announce that here was, 'One for the boys from the Rebel County' and launch into *Banks of the Sullane*, an old ballad about young love thwarted set on the banks of the river that flowed through Seani's hometown of Macroom.

Expectant eyes would fall on Seani, who had to observe correct protocol and acknowledge the honour done him by screwing his eyes closed in the pain of exile and covering his mouth with the hand that wasn't holding a pint lest trembling lip betray his emotion. At the tune's end, he made the formal expression of gratitude: 'Fair play to you, Harry. You're after getting me there. That song… The auld tunes… They'd bring a tear to the eye of a needle'.

As we left the little bar's yellow light and crossed the darkness into our truck cab, their soft voices singing Harry's ultimate homage to the late King followed us out into the night air that still smelled of that day's cut hay. Wood they get the words right this time or wooden they?

Can't you see I love you?
Please don't break my heart in two
That's not hard to do
'Cause I don't have a timber heart

We headed back slowly through Sixmilebridge where the lads would invariably still be out hurling on the old pitch in light that was fading as quickly and smoothly as if being turned down by a dial. Past the coffin-shaped graveyard and up the twisting climb to the long ridge of Cratloe and Gallows Hill at the top that fell down to Limerick just the other side. The wide Shannon estuary was at 12 o'clock straight-ahead and 10 miles away to the right in a deep space darkness was the constellation of Shannon Airport.

By now we were talked out, but even if we were chatting, we stopped, and looked at the bright lights of the airport the way a marooned Crusoe or Selkirk might look at the rescue fire they kept lit on some high point of their deserted island. Their fires were to alert passing voyagers but also to shore up the castaway's doubts about the possibility of rescue and purpose. The fire symbolised hope.

Shannon airport was our rescue fire. Obviously, it guided people in, but more important was the psychological role it played as a self-affirmation that we existed and had purpose; that we too in this obscure part of our obscure country were part of the wider whole. A wider world that was unimaginably different and exotic but which we could nevertheless access by the simple expedient of walking through the magic portal, the Star Trek Transporter, humming away somewhere within those lights.

We looked at Shannon Airport, but saw Boston or New York.

Because they began there: the airport wasn't us; it was an outpost of them. You came from Quin, went through the portal, and came out in Queens. The fact that we were looking at this hole in our space time continuum from the cab of our little truck after spending another day amongst the ancient boreens and eternal lakes of East Clare made more vivid the sensation that time only had real meaning – that the clock only really started – when you were there in the US suburb called Shannon Airport.

Out here – where we were – nothing really changed: As it was in the beginning, is now, and ever shall be, world without end. Down there was the Departure Lounge for Life, where in the words of another of Harry of Kilmurry's favourite songs *Spancil Hill,* you stepped on board a vision, the jet engines screamed, and you followed with the wind.

It was so much more than an airport.

That's why all the families from Limerick and Clare would drive out on Sundays and park their cars at the perimeter to look in wonder. They might get out and stand on the edge of the runways. Touching things and satisfying themselves that The Airport, our signal fire – the Star Trek Transporter that could beam us from Planet Potato back to USS Enterprise – was still there. That it hadn't just understandably got bored itself and decided one day that it too wanted to see a bit of the world and the bright lights of anywhere else.

We all went out to check that it was still there because we couldn't imagine that there wouldn't come a day when the airport itself didn't think, 'fuck this for a game of soldiers', check itself in and just take off – whiskey, frisky, let's get risky – and rise from the Green up through the Grey and up into the Blue, before banking westwards and out over the sea towards some place, any place... with a bit of action.

We had gone out to the airport on Sunday afternoons with all the other families and marvelled at the modernity. The clear tannoy announcements, the supersize trolleys, the girder sized Toblerones, chefs with real chef's hats like they had on television, baggage carousels, an elevator in which families shyly took turns going up and down.

Seani would say cite these things in support of his thesis – centred on Cork's mastery of the mysteries around the production of Hadji Bey

Turkish Delight – that there was nothing the Irish couldn't do if we took a right run at it. There was nothing stopping us only ourselves.

We went out one time to wave his Aunty Babe off back to San Francisco. On her head and in an almost certainly unintentional nod to the hallucinogenic Flower Power then associated with her adopted home, she wore a close-fitting white skull cap that tied under the chin and was covered completely with artificial yellow chrysanthemums.

Underneath the hat she had on those Gary Larson cartoon American ladies' glasses that angled up from the bridge of her nose at 45 degrees. On the drive home, Seani said that between the delta-winged specs and her hat, it was like looking through the windscreen of Concord and seeing the star of those Hollywood water ballets, Esther Williams, behind the airplane controls.

He didn't know why she'd wasted money on a plane ticket; if she walked out on the airport runway and angled her glasses to catch a good gust coming down from Cratloe and the Clare Hills, she could have glided back to the Golden Gate.

8

Maxi, Dick and Twank

(with special guest star, the ghost of Kenneth Williams)

IT IS A precarious thing to try and isolate the exact moment when you become sexually aware. For boys at least, there seems to be no 'exact moment', no sudden metamorphosis, instead a growing sexual awareness slowly takes you in its grip and compels you to begin taking yourself in a grip (as it were). That looking all around you gradually see, and that this whole new dimension to existence gradually superimposes itself over everything else and becomes the context within which everything must now operate. That you seem to have visited a universal optician who, having tested you on his phoropter (phoarr!) has given you lenses through which you will now view the world; a lens in which some outlines and shapes are so much bolder and present themselves so much easier.

All this is presented as happening in instalments, with lots of 'ing' present perfect continuous verbs to illustrate that it was an ongoing process and something both natural and life affirming: sap ris-ing, buck lep-ing, balls drop-ing

And yet my own sap rose and started overflowing like a broken tap all within a single Christmas Eve. The whole momentous change was telescoped into the 248 minutes it took my 13 years-old self to watch RTÉ's feature film *Cleopatra*. By the end of four hours – and out of nowhere – I was hopelessly in love with Elizabeth Taylor. And it wasn't what you'd expect; her asp or famous pyramids, it was her kohl-ringed eyes. I thought I'd never seen anything as amazing and, to this day, 40 years later, I can recall the dizzying, beautiful, all-consuming disorientation I felt as the blood drained from my head downwards to work the hydraulic sap riser. I was absolutely infatuated, but it was a courtly, chaste and unsullied kind of infatuation, less about lust than adoration and that kind of intense chivalrous desire to kill someone – or even better, be killed yourself – to prove the unquenchable purity of your ardour.

I fantasised about some furious sword fight in her defence during which I would receive a fatal but notably non-facially disfiguring head wound that allowed me a last few precious moments of shallow breathing and whispered, dry-lipped professions of devotion till my noble head, resting on her Nefertities, slowly turned to fix a glassy stare on some unseen presence.

As she beseeched me to live, I would reach out, every exertion an agony, to take the invisible proffered hand. In the instant my spirit leaves, I would stiffen dramatically before becoming limp (Ghost of Kenneth Williams: 'Haven't we all, Dear!')

Still holding my lifeless form, her screams of anguish would echo through the palace and her trembling bejewelled fingers would gently close my eyes. She would sob as she placed my head on the marbled floor with unimaginable gentleness, hysterical with loss and the realisation that the real love of her life had been beneath her controversial nose and unacknowledged all along.

I was indignant, too, by the way Cleopatra had been let down by her lovers. Harrison hadn't sorted anything out before it took 15-odd conspirators stabbing away for 10 minutes to let the air out of his Julius Caesar. Richard Burton was just too distracted by the Mary Quant mini-toga the costume department had him wearing. I particularly remember him falling on his sword because that night – still dreaming of Elizabeth Taylor and, unaware that my sap had well and truly risen – I flipped over to sleep on my stomach and nearly impaled myself.

The mid-70s cruelly exposed the gap that had always existed between Liz Ptolemy and Liz Hilton-Wilding-Todd-Fisher-Burton-Burton. It was hard for me (Ghost of Kenneth Williams: 'I'll bet it was!') to keep Liz up there on the pedestal when I could see her in my mother's *Evening Press* and *Daily Express* dragging a conspicuously porkier version of herself around Gstaad and Capri with old teensy toga himself, constantly looking pissed and wearing his 'n' her furs.

I was still fixated on having my sore head cradled on a dusky bosom and that was the cleavage from which emerged Peggy, the gorgeous, black, secretary to TV detective, Joe Mannix. Most episodes involved Mannix walking through doors and being pistol-whipped, to then regain consciousness with his head nestled on Peggy's pillows while she dabbed his brow and called his name anxiously. I read later that Mannix was knocked out 55 times over the course of the eight series and shot no less than 17 times, so actress Gail Fisher's chest was actually the most used prop during the whole series.

Fisher's part had originally been offered to the even more beautiful Nichelle Nichols, who had declined because she had already committed to *Star Trek*, where she played phasers-to-stunningly smouldering Lieutenant Uhura and deployed a couple of vulcans at an angle that demonstrated that, indeed, there was no gravity in space.

I knew that this was different to the way I'd felt about Liz Taylor. With her, I always felt like going down on my knees before her. With Lieutenant Uhura, and for some reason not yet apparent to me then, I always felt like having her on her knees in front of me. As I studied Uhura dealing with the excitable Scotty and the inscrutable Spock in her trim, Starfleet, standard issue communication's officer cocktail waitress dress, I would experience the by-now increasingly familiar feeling that had the blood draining out of my head, and heading off to itself boldly go to an extremity where no blood had gone before.

Show clips of these pneumatic characters accompanied by their show's theme music played non-stop at the edge of my every waking moment. Unless I was actively thinking about something else with a cold-sweat concentration – or even if I was and for a nanosecond my focus dipped below reactor core intensity – they sashayed into centrestage of my consciousness and effected a coup de tête. Every thought I had that originated or dealt with anything besides them seemed to know it had but seconds to make a case, stammering and falling over words in a frantic bid to convince me of its importance and relevance, nervously glancing to just off-stage where Liz Taylor drummed those lovely bejewelled fingers impatiently on her golden throne atop the life-size sphinx and adjusted her gilded bosom, before giving her ceremonial pharaonic flail a little whisk to announce that it was time for her to make another grand entry and that whatever was occupying my consciousness at that instant had better get out of the way or die screaming beneath the heavy tread of her Nubians.

The other message was that I had better go somewhere private where I could give my own ceremonial flail a rather more prolonged whisk.

Securing the five minutes of privacy necessary for a successful whisk in the Ireland of the 70s was not a humdrum affair. Families were much larger, and houses were much smaller. It was unusual for a child to have their own bedroom and positively rare for a boy. The norm in the standard three-bedroomed houses was a room for the boys, a room for the girls, and a room for mammy and daddy.

Traffic within the house was non-stop and boisterous. Internal doors were never closed, except for the toilet, and even there, the fact that most houses only had one toilet and the ubiquity of boiled cabbage in the national diet meant even getting five minutes in there without an urgent knocking on the door and a shouted demand to know how much longer you'd be, was practically unheard of. The toilet – apparently the sanctuary in other anglophone cultures for a leisurely uninterrupted whisking – was, in that Ireland, only slightly less busy than the nerve-centre, canteen, boxing ring, boardroom, court of law, surgery, interrogation room, teller's desk and CEO's office of the household: the kitchen.

Our toilet was right beside the kitchen so that users could continue to contribute to conversations being held around the table without having to shout, and the situation was commanded by a subtle etiquette that had the chat suspended the moment a note of strain was detected in the voice from within, and then smoothly resumed after the watery plop announced that the person within could now refocus their attention.

Invariably ,the person emerging had to squeeze past another entering, the whole discussion continuing now joined by the flush and the gurgling re-filling of the cistern. The toilet was in non-stop usage and I'd hazard a guess that I didn't sit on an entirely cold toilet seat till I was 10 years old. When my elder sister hit her teens and took up semi-permanent residence in the toilet so that she could use its mirror and sink, the door-hammering and 'last-helicopter-out-of-Saigon' tumult and crowd control issues reached the levels of permanent civil unrest. Seani decided to get some lads from Clare to build an extension to the house that would have as its centrepiece a second facility.[5]

In the meantime, I had my own involuntary and practically non-stop extensions to worry about and the possibility of retiring to the bathroom or anywhere else in that house for the few minutes of quietude necessary to make a sacrifice to Cleopatra Taylor on the several occasions an hour she demanded it was impossible. On top of the lack of opportunity there

[5] He announced that we'd be putting in a shower as well and a Greenshields Stamps brochure was sought that set out the range available by illustrating the different models all being used blissfully by a vaguely nude woman behind heavily frosted glass. Within two days of its arrival by post, the pages featuring the showers were mysteriously stuck together and had to be separated by sliding knives between the pages. But much useful information was lost in these rips and I've always felt a little guilty and responsible for the supernaturally shite choice they eventually made and described in 'The Taste of Pandy and the Smell of Benji'.

was my hopeless technique. I hadn't worked out how to take matters in hand and so instead settled on a move that kept the, er, ceremonial whisk itself stationary while moving the whole body around that fixed point in a laborious circle. In a striking coincidence, this was in planetary terms a Ptolemaic model where the celestial body moves around the fixed point of the earth.[6] It worked but was monumentally awkward, demanding a flat surface and plenty of room for the revolution around the fixed point.

The Copernican revelation where I discovered that rather than moving the whole body around the fixed point, it was plausible – and unimaginably more convenient – to move the fixed point itself and leave the rest of the much larger body stationary remains the single most useful application of a scientific principle I ever absorbed.

Enlightened thus, I was now able to relieve the situation without the whole palaver of theatrical yawns, followed by an airy announcement that I might go in for 'a little lie down'. I'm sure I did think that nothing untoward had been noted and that The Change that had come over me had escaped everyone's notice. And it probably had escaped everyone's notice except... The One.

A photo story-booklet by a Catholic society called (if memory serves) 'There's one part of boys that God doesn't want to stand up for His Faith' started magically appearing around me. At my elbow. When I turned around. In my way. I'd have to move it to get to something. In the drawer where I'd have to rummage for the Sellotape or shoelaces. Amongst the records, often right beside the 1975 *Top of the Pops* with the beautiful girl in the yellow leotard on the cover that had, purely by coincidence, an opening track called *Purely By Coincidence*.

I didn't believe then – and I don't believe now – in that kind of coincidence. So, still unsure whether I was dealing with numerous copies

---

[6] Ptolemy, 2nd century Egyptian astronomer and mathematician, descendant of the famous Greek pharaonic family. Most famous for his geocentric model of the universe set out in his seminal Almagest, which has had notable proponents including Frank Sinatra. Pto-le-my/ Why not take Ptolemy?

of the same pamphlet or a single copy with some supernatural capacity to appear in different locations simultaneously, I discreetly marked one of the pages and placed it exactly as if it had been carelessly tossed aside

A few hours later when a possible five-minute window opened up in the toilet's 24/7 booking and operations schedule, I decided to avail of the opportunity for the kind of dual-purpose visit now given the technical description of a 'shwank'.

Just as I sat down on the still-warm toilet seat, I noticed that there was no toilet roll left. Thanking Jesus that I hadn't been left – as so often before – in a postpartum situation where you had to ask someone outside to bring some toilet rolls to the door while they snickered and loudly talked over your increasingly plaintive pleadings, I went to the cupboard where I knew the household stock was kept.

There was a copy of the booklet.

Right there on top of the cellophaned jumbo pack. But was it the *same* copy? I turned to page 10 where 'John' was using his rosary beads as a tourniquet to cut the blood supply off from his own little demon. There it was.

The microscopic tear that I had put at the bottom of the page. This was the same booklet. But how could they have known that I'd have to come *here* unless they knew that I'd be going *there* and making the precautionary check for *this*? Someone was watching me. *Someone knew.*

The instant I knew that someone knew, I knew who that someone was. There was only person in our family that had that omnipotent power and knowledge. There was only one person that had that magical ability to see and not be seen. It was in my family – the same as it was in every other Irish family – the mother, the mam. The one who knew – not to mind what you were doing – but what you were thinking. And, moreover, what you were going to think. Where the chain of your thoughts would bring you, before you'd even recognised the first link, before you'd even realised you were involved in some mental process or sequence. You didn't even know you'd started, and she already knew where you'd end up and every little twist in the journey you'd take to get there.

There followed a really intense and life-changing lesson in operating and maintaining triple-bluff and the need for absolute impassivity, to betray nothing and to show no sign when you are being checked and moved imperceptibly but inexorably towards checkmate – and both you and your opponent know it.

I knew that she knew. Was it to my advantage to let her know that I *knew* she knew? How did that change the dynamic? Was it too early to show my hand? (Ghost of Kenneth Williams: 'Well, for Gawd's sake, make sure you're not holding anything!')

It was convoluted and Le Carresque: *Tinker, Tailor, Masturbator.*

I decided to convey, in an oblique way that also had the crucial component of deniability, that I knew that she knew. I waited a day or two and then, with an exaggerated nonchalance that I knew she'd pick up on, I went into the boys' bedroom with a record tucked under my arm. I had already taken the '75 *Top of The Pops* out of its usual place in the record player cabinet and hidden it in a spidery corner of the shed that she'd never go near. I made sure she heard my whistling exit from the room just a bare 30 seconds later – a period within which no man who ever lived would have been able to get one off.[7]

Out of the corner of my eye, I caught her, out of the corner of her eye, clocking the fact that I was now without the record. I called in a loud 'Bye' and slammed the front door shut. I guessed she'd go immediately to find the album which I'd obviously stashed away as a visual aid for use later. Naturally, she'd check underneath the blankets on my bed and that was where I'd put one of Seani's beloved Arthur Tracy albums, reverse side up, with just the tiniest and faintest line underneath one of the song

[7] **Maybe George Melly? 'My Canary Has Circles Under His Eyes'. I'm not fucking surprised.**

titles listed... *The Masquerade Is Over.*

When I returned later and checked the album, it was exactly where I'd left it but had been joined by a very old Decca single by the same singer, entitled... *It's A Sin To Tell A Lie.*

On the broader question, I am increasingly of the opinion that a whole generation of Irishmen is due a formal apology from the Irish state for its role in depriving them of any kind of healthy, normal, masturbatory material. Obviously, we do not mean anything like the current situation where eye-popping porn is now an environmental element, like carbon or oxygen.

We mean that no-one would have lost face and it would not have endangered the moral health of the nation had Ireland pretended to have a naturist movement, similar to those that flourished in Germany and Scandinavia, and permitted the sale and circulation of magazines like *Health & Efficiency*, featuring dumpy-but-enthusiastic housewives playing volleyball on a Baltic beach. Instead of even this concession to reality, Irish boys were condemned to brain-frying and deviancy-forming resorts to sun holiday brochures, advertisements for bath salts and 'how-to' wallpapering manuals showing women how to safely straddle stepladders.

Are we any better off for producing a generation of Irishmen amongst whose formative sexual experiences will be the frantic search in that relentlessly non-private world for a quiet corner and five uninterrupted minutes in which to consult a pattern book for crocheting bikinis?

Of course, the reason why so many now middle-aged Irishmen were gently warped in this way, where something as literally homespun (if odd) as knitting a woman's swimsuit is associated with feverish, every-second-counts, cross-eyed autoerotic stimulation to a background of parental roaring ('Where's he gone with the scuttle of coal?') is because of the insanely predominant voice played by the Church in deciding what did and did not constitute a proper understanding of the role that the sexual urge played – or rather, should play – in the lives of a Catholic society.

It was they who decided on the removal of any image that acknowledged the sexuality of the female form. Faced with questions about what did constitute acceptable cinematic entertainment for young Catholic boys, it was they who recommended the three-hour biblical epic in typically deranged belief that we'd be paying attention to Victor Mature's Samson or Charlton Heston's Moses, when we were actually taking mental screenshots of the dancing girls or Rita Hayworth's Salome. Considering the punishment the good book has God reserving for Onan for 'spilling his seed', it's always been a delicious irony that has the biblical epics of the 50s and 60s probably responsible for more spilled seed in His favourite little island than every blind farmer since the dawn of time.

An even more exquisite unintended consequence were the numberless fine young Irishmen who, desperate for a glimpse of a snow-white bosom barely restrained by a low-cut peasant blouse, had to lock horns with the demon princes presiding over the images of virgin sacrifice on the covers of Denis Wheatley novels and other occult-inspired pulp paperback tales. Naturally, we felt some religious trepidation at having to resort to the front cover of *The Devil Rides Out* or *To the Devil A Daughter* for a glimpse of a semi-naked woman and so had to develop a bifocal capacity that allowed you to see the image but not the words.

There was nothing that could knock you off stroke like suddenly looking past the sacrificial naked girl on the front cover and seeing the pentangle-adorned goat lord across whose outstretched hooves she lay and whose yellow eyes were looking straight out at you. When we had been told that this act – the very act in which we were now engaged – was to be considered a sacrifice to the Goat-Devil and that he liked nothing more than to clap along in time, his hooves sparking together in sulphurous rhythm.

Imagine the torrent of impulses and contradictory thoughts running through our young mind while thus engaged. The parts of our brains that dealt with sex and shame and fear and guilt lighting up and changing colour like Poundland fibre optic lamps. If that isn't enough psycho-static to be dealing with, why not put some doom-laden Black Sabbath in there to cover any sounds that might alert bat-keen maternal ears? Finally, behind even that, don't forget your father downstairs roaring out for the scuttle of coal that you were sent out '25 minutes ago' to bring in.

Would a *H & E* photospread of Birgitta and Helga playing with their beachball and letting the sun and wind air out their nooks and crannies not have been much more calming and more conducive to mental health? Would it not also have been, in theological terms, sounder?

It's all too late for these questions now. The question of whether it was right to have generations of young Irishmen trapped in this Paddylovian conditioning where they were erotically triggered by the sights of bath salts, a bottle of suntan lotion or just hearing the word 'Playtex' is purely academic now, and even then was on the verge of being overtaken by a television show set in the world of the Texas oil industry and responsible for more gushers than Standard Oil.

You hear a lot now about the seismic changes wrought by Fianna Fail's shattering defeat of the incumbent coalition in 1977. In socio-cultural terms, nothing of significance changed. It is the General Erection that occurred the following year when RTÉ began showing *Dallas* that actually begins Ireland's slow pelvic thrust into normal sexual imagery and association shorn of any pretence. The legendary soap-drama was set in Texas and revolved around the Ewings, a family with a wild-catting approach to the business of oil exploration and laying pipelines and a tom-catting approach to the business of keeping their biological pipes free-flowing and obstruction free.

The moment, the very instant, that Irishmen clapped eyes on Pam Ewing something stirred in the national groin. By Season Three when the opening credits had her advancing jiggling towards the camera, the sales of the *Evening Press* and *Evening Herald* doubled on the day the show was broadcast as thousands of helpless men and boys were forced to artfully arrange the opened journals into paper pup tents on their laps to disguise their own little drilling rigs.[8]

An extra frisson came from the fact that *Dallas* on some deep psychological level presented us with the classic erotic combo: lust and loss. That city, that name, that word, was already sacred to the tribe, but it represented mourning. JFK's picture was in most houses, usually alongside Pope John XXIII and often, depending on who the family had sided with in '22, either Dev or Collins. The new association of *Dallas* with desire or lust worked on the same ultra-sensual level of seeing a beautiful girl at a funeral mass and drifting off to imagine the magic bullets that would be her nipples or the various triangulations down to her grassy knoll, before the sound of the congregation standing or kneeling called you back to what you were meant to be thinking about.

Right behind Pam and as close as her freakshow bust-to-height dimensions would permit was Lucy Ewing who sparked a taste for pocket-sized and rocket-bosomed Venuses that would find its most popular expression in the person of Sam Fox, a 'Page Three Stunner' with strong Irish family connections that belied her Cockney tones and whose outsize Bristol Cities appearing almost daily in *The Sun* caused the most sustained period of Irish wire-pulling since rural electrification.

She was to prove the first and most enduring of a whole parade of Traceys, Sharons, Debees, Donnas, Belindas, Melindas, Suzis, Karens, Corinnas, Carinas and Marinas whose rise to perky omnipresence in the easily available British tabloids marked the decisive step in transitioning the boys of Ireland to normal sexual stimuli and away from the punji-traps of perversity that were the illustrated ads for reinforced gusset

[8] At the height of show's popularity – and the national horn it inspired – the Sunday World, the only native 'redtop' tabloid took a very deep breath and published topless pictures of a pre-Pam Victoria Principal. It has gone into legend as Palm Sunday.

ladies' jodhpurs in *Horse & Hound* magazine and missionary society annuals reporting on progress from deepest, darkest, topless, Africa.

It is the most graphic illustration possible of how precarious and shameful was the psycho-sexual ledge on which we had allowed ourselves to become stranded, that it took 'them next door', the most unabashed sexual deviants in Europe, to abseil down via elasticated ropes attached to nipple clamps and, gathering us to their redcoat gimp suits, carry Paddy towards safer sexual ground, calming and reassuring us by humming the theme to the *Benny Hill Show* as tunefully as the wedge of orange stuffed in their mouth would allow.

In an age when lads can climb to the summit of Ben Bulben, tap their phone three or four times and see and hear Ben Dover tapping his way through the Horney Housewives of Harlow, the idea of having to recognise, filch and then hide very tangential 'visual aid' material for the purposes of stress relief must seem as archaic a concept as having to go around the front of cars and vigorously rotate a hand-crank to a spluttering start was to us. If today they feel like hand-cranking to a spluttering start, they just pick up their phone. They don't have to forensically razor-remove a magazine page that featured an ad with a soapy woman endorsing a bath towel fabric softener and then carefully smudge the sequencing of the page numbers – like 'someone I know' once did.

Now those times and attitudes and requisite counter-surveillance skills are all tucked under the mattress of time and pushed very far back, never more to be taken out and consulted with a concentration no less diminished for having been done a hundred times before, that week. But that's the way of it; the sap that rose at the sight of Cleopatra all those years ago and solidified to an existential resin has become viscous again and is retreating down to the racy soil from which it sprang. I'm getting old now and am closer to the end than to the beginning.

But they have not grown old, as we that are left have grown old. They are still perky and beautiful, still 34-24-34, still mainly from Rochdale. At the going down of The Sun and in the morning's softer glories, we will remember them. I see them all now, not just Debbie and Debee and Debby, but all the goddesses to whom I made such frequent and intense recourse: the laughing stripper in the fur bikini straddling the crawl-tunnel into the igloo featured on my treasured miniature *Eskimo Nell* film poster. Victoria Cannon, the lustrous Latino from *The High Chaparral* who sounded as if she should be mounted outside the Imperial War Museum (and God help me, I would have). Pam Ewing, to whom I dedicated on a Dealy basis, the tantalisingly outlined model behind the frosted shower glass in the Greenshields Stamp brochure, the voluptuous dancing silhouette in the closing credits of *Tales of the Unexpected*, the girls who modelled the crocheted bikinis in *Woman's Way*, Farah Fawcett who put a Fossett's tentpole in our Farahs, and Ireland's answer to *The Supremes*, Maxi, Dick and Twank.

And Elizabeth Taylor. *Elizabeth Taylor.*

About 10 minutes into *Cleopatra*, just after the two-rolls-too-many rug reveal, Liz Taylor and Rex Harrison are fencing over precedence; she insults his maps, he sneers that she can brief his general staff. She realises that he is annoyed and in a matter-of-fact way that speaks of her incomprehension with the concept, she tries to apologise.

'We've gotten off to a bad start. I've done nothing but rub you the wrong way.'

Jesus.

All I wanted all my life was for Elizabeth Taylor to rub me the wrong way.

9

Tonight, There's Going to be a Jailbreak

I SUPPOSE WE were a musical family, insofar as we all loved music to varying degrees. We weren't one of those Irish families featured on RTÉ who upon finishing their evening Rosary pushed back the dresser, rolled up the rug, picked up whatever instrument daddy handed to them and bate out *The Maid Behind The Bar* while mammy hitched up her skirts to a daring mid-shin and pounded the boards while drying the dishes.

But we were no less slaves to the rhythm for that. We had an old Pye radio cabinet with a record player that was concealed under a hinged top, and which had a feature that allowed the heavy vinyl discs to be stacked and played automatically in succession. Seani had been given it as a present for his 21st in 1953 by his adoring mother and it represented an almost unimaginable technological 'lep' for the times.

In the same way as our kids now amuse themselves by watching us frantically pressing every button on our phones after they've sneakily cut into the kitchen Bluetooth speaker on which we'd been Spotifying, he had amused himself by using the hidden turntable to play his favourite record *The Desert Song* loudly and then watching any neighbours within earshot darting in to frantically twiddle their wireless dials away from the cosy domesticity of 'Athlone' and range across the European ether vainly trying to locate the station on which Maria Lanza anticipates gangsta-porno rap in *The Riff Song*.

Ho, we sing as we are riding.

Seani liked Jussi Björling, Paul Robeson, Orthurr Tracey, Jeanette MacDonald and Nelson Eddy. Lady Fecky's tastes went more towards Sinatra, Ella, Tony Bennett, and Sarah Vaughan whose name she would always preface with 'The Divine'. Both loved the classic American musicals of the 1950s and early 60s and we had all the albums often sung by the original Broadway cast. In the absence of even a car radio, any journey longer than 20 minutes involved a compulsory singalong medley of MGM's finest that was invariably kicked off with *Little Nellie Kelly* but would go much deeper than any kind of *Greatest Hits* superficiality and could deep-dive to obscure numbers that the Musical Director (herself) deemed apposite.

The twisty, tiring and breakdown-prone drive from Limerick down to our relations in Macroom would begin with a quick spoken 'Hail Mary' that we wouldn't get a puncture and then a more realistic risk-estimation through a note-perfect group rendition of *Cockeyed Optimist* from South Pacific. If we passed a carnival or any kind of open-air celebration in Kanturk or Millstreet on the way down or up, she pointed at it out the window and proclaimed: '*State Fair*' which was the signal for a segue into *It Might As Well Be Spring*. A merry-go-round at the carnival queued up *Carousel* and a heartfelt version of the Shirley Jones – Gordon McRae duet *If I Loved You*.

The unlikely event of being given something to eat in Macroom beyond a cold tay was contemplated longingly via *Wouldn't It Be Loverly* from *My Fair Lady*. An audible fart from one of the kids in the back precipitated a rootin' tootin' six-shootin' version of *Just Blew In From The Windy City* from *Calamity Jane*. When Seani noted the steep hill near

Macroom on which as a toddler he had learned to cycle by being helped up on to the bike and then launched from the top, we might break into competition with four opting for *The Black Hills* from *Calamity Jane* while three dug in with crampons to *Climb Ev'ry Mountain* from *The Sound of Music.*

I loved those tunes and love them still.

But every generation needs its own music, or at least its own twist on the existing canon and Captain Sensible and his post-punk revisionist version of *Happy Talk* was several years in the future. There was a degree of urgency about my quest to find my musical tribe as well. In the Ireland of the late-70s – certainly in the Limerick of the late-70s – teenage boys who were overheard singing *I'm Just a Girl Who Can't Say No* in the wrong circumstances could very easily find themselves in a turrible fix. It wasn't necessarily where a teenage boy wanted to be in terms of either musical self-identification or physical self-preservation.

The radio wasn't going to be giving you any answers either: Peters and Lee, who were on heavy rotation on RTÉ radio, were an Alan Partridge version of Ray Charles and Aretha. There was The New Seekers, Roger Whittaker and his whistle (which was so famous it was credited separately and had its own agent), Johnny McEvoy, Red Hurley, Sandi Shaw.

Vince Hill was Coventry's answer to Dean Martin, Joe Cuddy was Killester's answer to Coventry, Charles Aznavour was France's answer to Killester, Joe Dolan was Mullingar's answer to everything. They all warbled away in the very considerable shadow of Demis Roussos, the Greek singing lookalike for the then most popular wrestler in Britain (and son of Mayo emigrants), Martin Ruane, aka 'Giant Haystacks'.

Roussos had a soaring tremolo voice deployed to devastating effect in the anthemic *Goodbye, My Love, Goodbye* and *Forever and Ever* and his overwrought and thin 'Zorba the Irish Tenor' quiver was insanely popular in the musical home of the quivering tenor voice. He was able to put away his moussaka and his normal attire of circus big tops recycled into kaftans was a cause for some comment, but amongst a people who regarded 'trapped' wind as a dangerous, possibly fatal, threat to physical wellbeing, the claims of companionship he made in his *My Friend The Wind* guaranteed acclaim and an adoring public.

Greece was having a real moment because his only rival in terms of popularity and ubiquity on the radio airwaves was his countrywoman, Nana Mouskouri, a librarian Aphrodite smiling weakly through Michael Caine's glasses and singing about *The White Rose of Athens* and the fact that you owed 10p for a late return of your last book borrowed. Whatever was left of the national radio airtime was filled by Janis Joplin after a couple of tweaks by the Irish Catholic Bishops Conference: Dana.

The key thing to understand is that we hadn't *Top of the Pops* on television. We barely had television at all, and a decision was taken at the highest levels that the little we had was certainly not to be frittered away on something like Showwaddywaddy, a shi-shi-shittier version of the already soiled Sha Na Na. RTÉ's decision to ignore mid-70s British glam-pop was a perfectly valid decision to take – and coincidentally the correct one. But at the time, the complete lack of any comparison left us perilously vulnerable to the curse of the Irish; the siren voices who say: 'Shure we'll have a go ourselves. How difficult can this be?'

The same people who heard about a salad niçoise and came up with the cold tay.

The musical equivalent of the cold tay were the showbands that traversed the country in transit vans. You could see advertisements for them in the papers and they all looked the same: jug-eared, centre-parted fellows, the older ones on the brass instruments, the younger ones on guitar and keyboards, the drummer was 'a character' (alcoholic with mental health issues). The youngest and best looking (decent thatch of hair and his own teeth) did lead vocals, while they all executed synced dance moves that The Temptations or The Pips might have thought were a physio routine for recovering stroke patients.

Remember that these lads were the 'youthful' end of the Irish popular music spectrum. At the other end was traditional or ceili bands, with the middle being occupied by the groups that played afternoon dances and who, by convention, all featured such a preponderance of cross-eyed accordion players that a full half of the country routinely wondered aloud whether their own eyes were straight in their sockets when they looked at the band photo accompanying the advertisement for the coming Sunday afternoon's dancing in the 'The Smiling Shillelagh Hotel' in Borris, courtesy of Jimmy Kelly and Jamboree.

Wedged in there between the cross-eyed accordion players and the snare-drum propelled Phil Spector-ish 'Wall of Fiddles' that were the ceili bands were the Country 'n' Irish singers who hailed from the Midlands or North and who presented as various degrees of mutation from Marty Robbins. They specialised in that particularly clammy Irish version of motherlove that we can call O'Edipus, so *Mammy's Tears* or *Mammy's Last Words* or *A Mother's Blessing* or *The Only Time Mammy Touched Satin Was in Her Coffin*. They didn't so much sing as recite litanies of troubles and woes in a barely audible whiney baritone or bass set to waltz time, and besides mammy's fully justified trepidations and warnings to desist, their other obsession was anthems to their obscure homeplaces, so *Lovely Leitrim* or *Take Me Back To Termofeckin* or *I'm Boilin' To See Boyle*.

Their ultimate thematic scrabble score was their being taken home from the sweat of the building sites and the Galtymore to the sweet town of (insert name here) for mammy's funeral all set to the One-Two-Three melody of *The Galway Shawl* and lyrics that explained that *The Shovel that Dug Dulwich is Digging Mammy's Grave*.

In fairness to me, I had enough innate musical taste and awareness to know that if Showband, Afternoon Dancing and Country 'n' Irish were the alternatives to Lady Fecky and Seani's collection of Broadway musicals, then I'd stay hanging around 42nd Street. I didn't know what a lobby was – much less whether it needed washing down – and though we now realise that the song is a sex worker's invitation to pre-coital genital hygiene, even then I didn't want anything of mine washed down by anyone who had anything to do with this kind of shite.

God knows that any kind of run-up to sexual activity in that Ireland was mysterious and opaque enough without being hidden in language ostensibly intended to show people how to prepare rooms for wallpapering.

All of which left me no further along in my quest for a musical home. I needed some sign from above; someone or something that would set me on the right road.

The gods of Hollywood heard my prayer and gave me my mission. We were off to see the Wizard. And Bowie. And Slade. And Mud. And Roxy Music, Suzi Quatro and Hot Chocolate.

For a fortnight every Summer, we went to Dublin to see our grandmother and stayed with our cousins who all lived around Clonskeagh. The visits were chiefly marked by an almost manic determination on the part of Lady Fecky and her sister, Aunty Madge, to hit every national landmark and notable destination within a comfortable Hillman Hunter trundle of Stephen's Green. Every day we might hit off for the Pine Forest where we were encouraged to keep our eyes peeled for 'squirridles' or Avondale or Powerscourt or Newgrange or Saint Valentine's heart or Kilmainham Gaol (where Seani's mother and aunt had been imprisoned) or the GPO or the National Botanic Gardens or Howth Head ('Imagine if we saw Gay Byrne!') or Dublin Castle, within a flung chamber pot of which our great-grandparents had cobbled the officers' footwear that pressed so firmly on the national neck. My mother and her sister were early and enthusiastic advocates for the idea that would later be classified as 'infotainment', where learning and information might be smuggled into children disguised as entertainment. It was a revolutionary concept in Irish children's learning where the 'Pebbledash Principle' was still the orthodoxy: if you throw enough shit hard enough at a rough wall some of it will always stick.

As is usual in these kinds of cultural sheep-dips, what we were being dunked in was much less interesting than where the dunking took place. The national attractions we were told we should find fascinating were less fascinating than the unremarked upon background on which these national attractions were laid. To us from the wrong side of RTÉ's totalitarian Cathode Ray Curtin, the idea of the all-day television they had in Dublin was barely comprehensible and both unimaginably exotic and wonderful.

The idea of multiple choice of all-day channels was an orgasmic advance on something already sublime; like a pressed arctic explorer happening on a much-needed toilet in the middle of the frozen wastes and then discovering that the seat is heated.

Television was still then a fully exotic and vaguely interactive medium with older viewers talking directly to the characters and about them to the other people in the sitting room. My granny, Lady Fecky's mother, watched the wrestling, stamping her foot and doing air-chokes while she urged on Big Daddy during his weekly matches with Demis Haystacks/Giant Roussos and Mick McManus. Loud partisanship and running commentary on what was being viewed was not just tolerated, but deemed as integral to the whole experience as the programme itself. There was no recording or rewind facility, so as people left and re-entered the room the onus was on the last person who had received an update to update the newest viewer. The original viewer – the only one who actually knew the whole story – was exempt from providing updates because they were deemed to be too involved in the story to be expected to take time out to explain to latecomers what had happened.

People think that the National Question in Ireland in the 1970s referred to the slow-motion massacre that was daily occurring in the Six Counties. Actually, the National Question in that Ireland was the one asked 20 times a night in every house on every road whenever someone re-entered the room where the television was on.

Did I miss anythin'?'

Our cousins' house in Clonskeagh was no different. Except for one programme. Only one programme was viewed and listened to in a monastic silence. That programme, ironically, was *Top of the Pops* broadcast on Thursday evening. Nobody could talk while it was on, and emergency piss-trips were to be on tippy-toe with the sitting room door opened by steady fast pull to minimise squeaks. Instructions given, my cousin Helen would ceremoniously place her tape recorder with its condenser microphone in front of the television set and as the BBC continuity announcer introduced the programme, she pressed 'Record'.

The first time, the very first time, I heard *Whole Lotta Love* I knew I had found my Riff Song. Nothing could be the same. Everything was changed. I'd been foolin', I needed schoolin'.

The bands featured in the countdowns teetered through my consciousness on their platform boots clothed in so much silver tinfoil that the only pop that could reasonably occur was into an oven on a low heat. Helen's favourite was Alvin Stardust, a dark smouldering K-Tel Heathcliff in Elvis's 1968 Comeback Special leather jumpsuit who pointed at us through the camera in gloved fingers festooned with bulbous poison rings. I liked the unsettling dark anguished feel to it all but I'd no idea what a Coo Ca Choo was ('Come on! Let's go to my flat/ Lay down 'n' groove on the mat') and just assumed that he was very keen on a brand of bubble-gum or a Hornby toy train.

I knew I was getting closer. If I could just find music with an unsmiling and slightly sinister feel, based around fuzzy guitar riffs and played by gloomy, pasty-faced Brits dressed in black and wearing rings and crucifixes ransacked from Liberace's jewellery box, then I was sure that my search for musical meaning would be over.

Hello, Black Sabbath.

My older cousin, Paul, was already filtering out the extraneous shades and tints from his life: his bedroom walls were painted a deep purple and he listened to King Crimson, Blue Oyster Cult and Sabbath – lots and lots of Sabbath. If he felt like something a little lighter, he put on Pink Floyd or Tangerine Dream. He liked that I had liked the Zeppelin riff that *Top of the Pops* used to trick people into looking at shite like The Rubettes, and he thought I had potential. But he explained how supremely important it was not to let Smokie get in your eyes. It was not possible for any of us to remain neutral in a conflict as elemental as this: I was at the first and most important of life's binary choices – because music was not just what you listened to; it was what you were. Deciding on your music was effectively deciding on yourself, who you wanted to be and how you wanted to be seen. It was a statement of Cartesian profundity: I listen to, therefore I am.

I could either go with Pop-groin and listen to 'light' chart music about meeting girls at the Friday night dance, being happy or sad and the real stuff of everyday life. Or I could go with Rock-brain and listen to 'heavy' music about imaginary worlds with a lot of Nordic swords and lightning bolt imagery that were inhabited by demons and in which the only girls were usually two-timing elves with intimidating granite bosoms and snakes coming out of their eye sockets and every other orifice.

Put that way, it's obvious that I should have stayed with Pop, after all there was only mere months to go before Punk kicked down the door and tinfoil suits and star-shaped guitars went the way of the dodo. But how was I to know? By the time that the 'Anarchy' sounded the chord that was heard around the world, I was already living musically and emotionally in a Yes or Uriah Heep album cover where pixies and sorcerers played out their eternal Tolkien duel.

Even at that late moment, I think I could have switched to Punk – they played power chords as well – but we never heard it. I'd check out the latest charts as soon as they were pinned up in the downstairs record department of the Limerick Eason's, it was like a cryptic crossword; how were we meant to know who The S** Pistols were when we barely knew what S** was in the first place? By the time, the Irish censors were finished with it, their debut album – the most important album of the decade – could have been retitled, *Never Mind the Letters, Here's the Asterisks.*

It's the story of a long and winding musical road not taken, if I'd checked out Helen's records I'd have stayed with Bowie and Roxy, wiped Punk's spit out of my eye, and then entered the golden age of British pop that waited just the other side: The Jam, Elvis Costello, Joe Jackson, Squeeze and The Pretenders, The Specials and the Byron of Holloway, Ian Drury. Instead, I went through Paul's records and took the fork in the road that brought me to the Denis Wheatley of Dudley, Ozzy Osbourne.

I could have gone through my formative years buying normal records with five tracks each side. Instead, I spent every last penny I had buying triple concept albums with two songs on each side, culminating in my buying an Emerson, Lake and Palmer triple live album with six songs in total on the whole thing. It was called *Welcome Back, my friends, to the show that never ends.* Truer words were never said.

I could have listened to those works of art that told us something about the human condition, like *Love Will Tear Us Apart.* Instead, and trying to hear disguised messages about the human condition and hidden salutations to the dark lords, I spent whole days slowly hand-spinning records backwards by bands from whom you were lucky to hear something fucking intelligible when you played their records forward at the correct speed.

Neither would I have made such a tool of myself by being unable to pass an open microphone without screeching out the stage announcements from favourite live albums to entirely confused small gatherings. What did the farmers at the local IFA meeting in Morrison's Lounge in Ballysimon think when I snuck up to the top table, picked up the microphone and lifting from the legendary

Strangers In The Night live album brought the meeting to order with a bellowed 'Hello, Chicago! Will you please welcome from England… U…F…OOOOO!!' Or warming up the crowd at the Monaleen Bridge club prize-giving night in the Castle Oaks Hotel with some of the audience-patter from Ted Nugent's 'Gonzo' Double-live: 'This guitar is guaranteed to blow the balls off a charging rhino at 60 paces. And now, a bottle of Winter's Tale sherry each to the best Novice Pair, Norah Casey and Peggy Leyden'.

And am I honest enough, even now, to admit that I would love to have been able to dance? That I would have given anything to have had the balls and balance to have asked a girl up to dance to *If I Can't Have You* which I secretly loved then – and still love now – but which, as part of my 'heavy' musical persona, I had to pretend to despise. I'd love to have been able to dance gracefully, glide and strike poses. Why did we never learn to dance? How insane was it that wanting to dance with girls was interpreted as effeminate?

Disco was in a category below even Pop. Village People we understood as a FAS or ANCO training and career agency put to a disco beat. You could be a sailor. You could be a cowboy. You could be a red Indian (why not?). You could be a hard-hat construction worker, something that we Irish were already genetically predisposed towards. You could be a postman and wear their uniform of leather pants and leather hat with mirror shades. You could join the navy and stay in some class of An Óige hostel called a 'YMCA' while you were making your mind up about your career. It all seemed straightforward enough. A friend confidently announced that Village People were 'queer' and, sure enough, we agreed that a postal service that encouraged their employees to wear leather pants and sport Mexican bandido drooping moustaches was indeed an odd thing.

But then we noted that the Americans probably thought the same thing about our lads ceaselessly shifting their dentures and the cheeks of their arse on the hard saddle of their bikes as they trundled around Ireland in low gear, up and down boreens, delivering the letters while fighting off Jack Russells and farm collies.

What really strikes me, looking back, was the fact that my younger brother, Gunga, didn't follow me in the fruitless search for the rhino's balls after they were blown off by Ted Nugent's guitar. It's fair to say I'd an undue influence on Gunga. He listened to me, and I tended to make the big strategic calls for both of us on the basis that I was older and that I read – he didn't read and accepted completely that this lack denoted an incapacity to strategise. So, I tended to advise him on what our joint positions on any issues was going to be and, up to this point, my decisions had been accepted without demur. But he wouldn't go with the metal and the wizards and the whole gloomy synthesiser and Moog peddle 'double-live' Dungeons and Dragons musical diarrhoea that I told him were the only records that should be permissible in our shared bedroom.

I was way ahead of him on certain stuff that no sensible teenage boy gave a fuck about anyway; I told him that if we wanted to understand Neil Peart's lyrics for Rush then we'd just have to get to grips with Nietzsche. He said he was equally certain that that was a make of Japanese power drill. When I noted the bravery of Judas Priest in having two lead guitarists up front, he waved a photo of Kate Bush wearing some clinging chiffon in front of me and roared that Kate had two up front that were much more worthy of admiration than two more beefy Brummies suction-packed into PVC leotards. Where were all the girls? He asked this indignantly and repeatedly.

'How come there's never any girls in these fucking records?' he asked through narrowing eyes.

Stung, I played him Phil Lynott's joke at the start of Emerald from *Live and Dangerous:* 'Is there anybody here with any Irish in them?

Would any of the gerrls like a little more Irish in them?'

Did he see now? Could he not hear Phil joking about doing the other thing with girls?

'But listen to the crowd roaring back. There are no girls there! I bet you there wasn't a girl within a fucking mile of the place. He's asking the girls would they like a little more Irish in them and all the lads seem to be roaring back that – shure as long as it's going – send a little their way. That's my exact point. You're making my argument', he triumphantly concluded.

He had a point, there was no denying the evidence of my own ears. I loved Lizzy and loved Phil. And maybe it's a bit unreasonable to have expected him to ask, 'In the highly unlikely event of there being any gerrls here, would they like a little more Irish in them?'

But then maybe the drugs that would rob us of our greatest hero were already there?

Tonight, there's going to be a jailbreak, somewhere in this town, he sang.

Jesus, Phil. I dunno. But my guess would be the jail?

Gunga was exactly right about the girls. This was all-male leather music without even the fun of being gay. I know it now and, honestly, I knew it then but was too far down the hole (up my hole?) to do a reverse-ferret.

He listened to Hall and Oates, George Benson, Motown, Marvin and Otis, Donna Summer and Stevie Wonder. Alongside that soul train, he had the Doobie Brothers' Long Train Running pulling a clean West Coast sound. He was obsessed with Fleetwood Mac and specifically with Stevie Nicks, holding the inner sleeve of *Rumours* in front of him and staring at the photos of her while he slowly twirled a lock of his hair in a do-not-disturb signal of deep focus. She was wholesome and sun-kissed, he explained. How could we not see how beautiful and golden she was?

Out of pure spite and still irritated that he had rejected my programme for our joint-enrolment in an intensive study of Yes concept albums, I told him that – speaking of rumours – the music press was convinced that his precious Stevie had a personal assistant whose chief duty was blowing something called cocaine up her landslide. What did he think of that? He said that so far from taking money, he'd pay her for the privilege of doing the job. Then he sang some rephrased lines from *Sara* about how he was the blowin in her arse.

I gave up. You have to know when you're wasting your time.

Anyway, I'd other lads to drag into the dry ice and drown.

I infected one pal so badly with Prog that he went around Ireland to find a copy of the rare Genesis concept double album *The Lamb Lies Down On Broadway* which he insisted on playing down the phone to me. After 20 minutes that felt like 20 days and could have been 20 years, I gave up, put the phone back in the cradle and promptly forgot about it. Seani went out to ring up about a funeral in Cork and stormed back into the room in a fury. Who had been on to the Speaking Clock and hadn't hung up properly? Did we think he was made of money? When I went out and gingerly picked up the phone, holding it away from my ear I could still hear Peter Gabriel singing *Counting Out Time*.

And it's easy now to feel embarrassed about having three Emerson, Lake and Palmer live albums, including one that was triple live itself and another one that was knob-twiddly interpretation of Mussorgsky's *Pictures at an Exhibition*. I still hadn't earphones and was listening to these hours of flatulent keyboard parping lying on my stomach with a stereo speaker positioned either side of my head and going as fucking cross-eyed in the process as the accordion players in the afternoon dance bands that I had laughed at. I knew that this must end in tears.

I had once loved hearing my mother, Lady Fecky, join in on Sabbath's *Sweet Leaf* while she was doing the ironing and not – as I boasted to impressed friends – just duetting with Ozzy on the screamed *Alright now!* at the start, but actually coming in on the manic pothead repeat-coughing introduction even before the first thunderous chords. I was proud of the way she had steered into the dark. She'd ask me to put on *Some Enchanted Evening* for her and I'd pretend to misunderstand, so instead of South Pacific, I'd put on the Blue Oyster Cult live album of that name. She'd continue peeling carrots and, shaking her head, begin to tell me that I was the greatest pain in the arse that ever... before she was drowned out by the drums announcing the beginning of *R.U. Ready 2 Rock* and, beat-perfect, she'd automatically slide into a Loreto choir soprano solo: *Come on, come on, to the stations of light/Come on, come on, everybody's waiting.*

But I didn't want to hear my mother joining in on *Cat Scratch Fever.* I didn't know what it was – neither did Ted Nugent, according to his lyrics – but I was pretty sure that whatever it was it didn't involve a trip to the vets. The day I heard my mother singing along to Aerosmith's *Back In The Saddle* was the day I fell off the heavy rock horse. A middle aged Irish Catholic mother had gone from *Annie Get Your Gun* to *I'm riding, I'm loading up my pistol/I'm riding, I really got a fistful.*

This had to stop. Whatever about ruining my own life, this corruption of innocence was unforgiveable and had to cease.

So, I started turning my music down from the 11 it had been at. I had a look at some of the Irish bands that might have filled the 20-minute drum solo-shaped hole in my being. Not for me. Not then. I couldn't get there.

People said try Horslips, but I wanted to leave the whole mists-of-time and moustache thing behind. They projected that Celtic mythological 'Book of Invasions' vibe, but I just got 'Asterix and Dearg Doom'. The other contenders were Moving Hearts, a nightmarish rendezvous of Prog, Jazz fusion and Trad all wrapped in beardy earnestness and musical virtuosity, a kind of Jethro Tulla Céilí band.

The only thing for it then was a slow decompression. Like those divers that come up from great depths and must wait for set periods at various levels on the way up so there's no possibility of nitrogen poisoning, I would have to come up slowly and pause at progressively more shallow levels of music till the possibility of poisoning was gone entirely. Remember that I had bought, listened to, and loved *Budgie – Live in Los Angeles* and try and grasp the fact that they were a Welsh band usually classified as a Heavy Metal Tom Jones.

That's a long way down. That's deeper than the Mariana Trench. And even as I write that, I've to wonder if there wasn't a band called 'Mariana Trench' and did I not have their double-live? That's how deep I was. It's a wonder I ever got back up at all.

But I did. Now I've a perfectly normal relationship with music and can listen to Bananarama or Robbie Williams on those 'Gold' or 'Classic' stations without suffering near-fatal acid reflux or experiencing an almost irresistible urge to kill all around me.

People who know the stygian depths to which I had fallen, with the wizards and concept albums and minute comparison of lights shows and whose stack of Marshalls was bigger, often ask me when I knew I was free. When I knew for certain that I need never again stare for hours at a photo of an inflatable pig floating over Battersea Station wondering what the fuck that was meant to signify but convinced that it *did* mean something because it *had* to mean something. The logical loop of all loopy beliefs

I always give them the same answer. The one I spurned all those years ago and which began my descent down, down, deeper and down. The one that Gloria had beseeched arrogant, know-it-all, me to heed way back then and which would have taught me humility and at least one single dance, the waltz.

One day at a time.

10

Old Spin and New Spin

Wayne Rooney's Hair on Mickey Rooney's Head

LOOKING BACK NOW, I'm not sure that people in that Ireland ever really got the concept of holidays or rather 'going on holiday'. I know that my father didn't. To Seani, not working constituted a holiday, so going away to *not work* was to add a superfluous layer of activity. If they lived in cities or larger towns, people sent their children back to grandparents for a fortnight of spiritual retreat engendered by nightly rosaries, and their annual digestive purges effected rudely by industrial scale consumption of cabbage water and milk straight from the churn.

The fortnights on the old family farm also had a Maoist cultural revolution role where suburban teenagers and children deemed to be 'too soft for their own good' or who wanted things 'nice and handy' were taught through a heavy schedule of turnip-snagging and shit-shovelling what hard work was. A month of back-breaking bale-stooking and sifting and sniffing calve scutter for worms wondrously focused young minds on the need to begin thinking seriously about the state exams that they'd be sitting in the five years that 'they wouldn't feel going'. The preponderance of South Kerry families in the Civil Service and teaching professions and their conviction that this aggressive agrarian 're-education' worked led to a whole generation of Dublin teenagers serving terms in this Kenmare Rouge chain of work farms.

The Irish idea of holiday was therefore a corruption of the American 'Same shit, different day' where it became 'Same shit, different house'. The idea of going somewhere to enjoy yourself by doing nothing was practically incomprehensible and if understood at all, was as a Platonic ideal; a purely internal concept apprehended by reason and formed by movies, books, and specifically, advertising.

No-one knew what JWT actually did, any more than we understood what all those other three-initials organisations like the CIA, KGB or the NHS did, but that wouldn't have been a cause for alarm or even curiosity. Ireland – particularly the northern part of it – led the world in mysterious three-letter groups that promised to give you an experience that you'd never forget and about which it was as well not to become too curious.

On both sides we were generationally too far out of our original farms in (his) Inchegeela and (hers) Skibbereen, and my mother, Lady Fecky, understandably wanted to spend time with her mother in her old home in Dublin. Every year in July we stayed with our cousins in Dublin for a week or fortnight in summer and often tagged along on their holidays which took them down the Sunshine Highway from Clonskeagh to Rush, a seaside village past Malahide and before Skerries. All of us crowded into what I remember as a modified Nissen hut constructed of corrugated iron and earwigs, where we listened to Mungo Jerry's *In the Summertime* and obliviously to The Kinks' *Lola* on heavy rotation on a cousin's tape machine, and consumed faddish variations on the classic seasonal 'Cold Tay' (Corned beef and tinned pineapple on cocktail sticks, who knew?). Very probably connected to this tampering with the old recipe, another cousin vomited spectacularly and in science-defying quantities while flying around on the outside seat of the carnival chairoplane. If I close my eyes, I can still hear the crowd's screams over the hurdy-gurdy's *Wouldn't You Like to Fly?* by 5th Dimension

There didn't seem to be any question of just our family going on a holiday. I can't ever recall a mention, much less a conversation. Like many men of his generation, Seani didn't 'do' holidays; he didn't understand them, and was, I think, embarrassed by his inability to work out what was going on and what he was meant to do. He didn't know how to do *nothing* and would have been self-conscious of how clumsy and fake his efforts would appear.

He had, as well, that indefinable sense that 'holidays' – as described and advertised by papers like those owned by that 'Orange bastard, Beaverbrook' – were not for us.

That, as commonly understood and on the national spiritual level which should be as familiar and easy for good Fianna Fail people like us as our own kitchen table, holidays were somehow un-Irish and to be avoided if not outright rejected.

The fastest way of finding if something was un-Irish on this existential level was to ascertain the English attitude to it. Did they do it and did they like doing it?

If the answer to those questions was that they did, then it was self-evidently something that we should not be doing and should be against, as a matter of principle. Any examination of English cult of the holiday with its landlady fumbling under the pier with George Formby's little stick of Blackpool Rock, donkey rides, the week in Margate, the windbreakers-as-battlements conquest and colonisation of a beach, had to conclude that this was indeed 'theirs' and therefore something of which we should be wary.

The way they sat on their deckchairs in their kiss-me-quick hats looking proprietorially at our sea and dreaming of new ways to piss-on-Paddy all confirmed that this kind of holiday was something they did and liked and, *ipso facto*, something we should not do and should be against. Irish people going on holidays in that way – *their* way – were revealing themselves as seaside shoneens.

Let the traitors ape their masters and go on their week's holidays to the seaside. We would remain true to the kind of vacation that Finn MacCool, Brian Boru, Hugh O'Neill, Bold Robert Emmett and Pearse would have chosen if they wanted to take some time off from defending Ireland's honour... we would go for a spin.

If right this moment you asked anybody under 40 years of age whether they wanted to go for a spin, I'd bet they would interpret that as asking them whether they wanted to join you for a session of frantic exercise involving roared commands from an instructor to serried ranks of men and women, all pedalling furiously on stationary bikes and sweating like bullocks.

In their Ireland, that's what they understand 'going for a spin' to mean.

But asking the exact same question in our Ireland meant, who wanted to go on a peculiarly aimless motorised excursion that not alone had no purpose but was advertised, specifically, on that basis. A drive that would be vague in every respect except the absolute certainties that, at some stage and regardless of season, it would involve sitting outside a pub till mammy sent one of the kids in to get daddy out and, in its summer variant, that all – including the driver who would almost certainly have had six pints in the hour just beforehand – would have a swim followed by mild sunstroke, while listening to a tinny transistor broadcasting GAA matches and eating Irish tapas: cold mashed turnip with a spoon of Branston's Pickle on a wilting cream cracker.

An announcement in our Ireland that 'a spin' was being considered ('Who wants to go for a spin?') was an exactly defined suggestion about an unbelievably vague activity. That 'spin' was a motorised dander; its defining characteristic was that you weren't going *anywhere*.

Oh, you were going, certainly. And you were going by car. But after that it was all up for grabs: you didn't know where you were going and – what's more – it didn't matter. That was the whole point. If the then Irish idea of 'going for a spin' was a song, it would be Chuck Berry's anthem to the open road but sung in waltz time by Danny Doyle or Val Doonican.

Driving along in my Vauxhall Viva
Five in the back and four in the front, if you can believa'
Taking turns to roll up and down the window
With no particular place to go

As it happens, I always liked going for spins in the old meaning. I always liked the 'As I roved out' vibe; the idea that we'd know where we were going when we got there. That the world – or at least that bit of it between Ballylongford and Banna in North Kerry – was your periwinkle.

Everyone else in Limerick headed west to Clare and Kilkee or Lahinch or Spanish Point. But our spins always went south to Kerry. Again, this was down to Seani. He thought the Clare and Limerick people fine and their taste in most matters no less true and only marginally less sophisticated than Cork people. But on the question of beaches, he was unswerving. There were no beaches in Ireland like the ones in Kerry. If they were good enough for Roger Casement, they should be good enough for anyone. And they were no further away than the ones in Clare. It was as broad as it was long, he would declare as breezily as the wind whipping in and bending the flakes in our 99s to a right-angle as we sat shivering on Nun's Beach in Ballybunion.

I'm not sure he was right about that, and I'm inclined to think there was something more psychologically elemental going on and resting on the indisputable fact that everyone prefers relieving themselves in their own bathrooms. Seani was quintessentially Cork and when the people of that place wade through the splashing crowd into sea up to their stomach to savour a sneaky, long, bracing, staring away at the horizon, hands-onhips, piss into the briny vastness, then they naturally want to be in the sea off Garristown or Inchydoney. If they can't be in Cork for that summer treat – and those beaches were too far away for a one-day spin from Limerick – then they want to do it in Kerry, God's last prototype before he achieved Paddy Perfection in Cork.

But his children were more Limerick than Cork and were becoming resentful – in the classic 'East is East' manner experienced by the second generation of immigrant families – of the way we were expected to spurn the tastes of our Limerick neighbours and friends in favour of our father's Cork and Kerry 'South is South' homeland culture. Why couldn't we go for a spin to Kilkee like everyone else on the road and in the parish? Why were we still the only ones in our part of Limerick that faithfully headed south-west through Askeaton and above Aughinish, down into and up out of the small gently sloping village of Loughhill, whose banked and curved main street facilitated a through-traffic speed that had the experience of a popular local analogy for uncontrollable diarrhoea: 'The dinner went through me like a wedding through Loughill!'

Kilkee was also the summer residence of a new lad who'd moved to our part of Limerick and with whom I had become fast friends. His dad was Jewish and from Leeds, while his mother was local and Catholic, and he announced that he was therefore the product of the two most dynamic races in the world. How this incendiary mixture would manifest itself, he was not yet able to confirm, but that it would, he – and after the briefest acquaintance, we – had no doubt.

We knew nothing about Judaism except that it involved circumcision of infant boys and genuinely curious, we asked him whether he had undergone the ritual. He proudly announced that he had and recommended it to any of us who wanted a 'good hard tip'.

He told us about his uncle in Leeds, who had had 10 sons and, as each was circumcised, he had carefully kept and stored the little foreskins which he had then commissioned a master tailor to sew into a purse for his coin change. Not alone was it perfectly suited to this role, but he explained that if you gave the purse a good rub it turned into a suitcase. He had an early model skateboard, was good at football and a sister in whose presence and for reasons I couldn't completely understand, I felt clumsy and tongue-tied. He seemed to exist on a more sophisticated level than we – certainly, I – did and even the fact that his family decamped to Kilkee for the whole summer in the manner of the Kennedys to Hyannis Port was fascinating and made our own 'Who wants to go for a spin?' mystery daytrip tours of Lixnaw look hopelessly naïve and provincial.

Why couldn't we go to Kilkee like everyone else? How was I ever going to present a more windswept and interesting version of myself to the sister? Surely, I'd be able to get out one single mildly interesting and coherent sentence in her presence, if I was there for a week or something? In Kilkee they played rackets on the beach and talked about bumping into Dickie Harris. They draped their jumpers over their shoulders while walking out to Burns or the Pollocks for nude swims. Grown men in Kilkee wore actual shorts; they didn't just roll the legs of their ordinary flannel or Farah pants up to knobbly knees. In Kilkee they knew that Ambre Solaire was not a response in the Latin Mass. Why couldn't we go there like everyone else from Limerick? What was the fucking mystery?

Nobody could give me an answer that made sense to me, and I began agitating, nibbling away at my mother, who, I knew, would have the last word on this – as she did on every question that she adjudged material to her children's happiness and welfare. I enrolled my younger and much more bolshy brother, Gunga, in the campaign and his expletive-peppered tirades against the present policy of aimless and time-limited 'spins' and eating gritty sandwiches on various North Kerry beaches was decisive. He was too old for that shite, he declared. He was nearly 12 and it was time for him to begin smoking, playing pool in the amusement arcades and getting into fights outside chippers.

Searching for the suitable analogy, he explained to my mother that holidays themselves were like a go on the seaside bumper cars. When you're small, stretching down to press the accelerator pedal left you too short to see right over the steering wheel, and it was 'a pain in the hole' but understandable that you might have to let one of those surly mute funfair workers stand on the back of your car and lean over you to do the steering. But there came a time in a man's life when people would be entitled to sneer at you for continuing to allow this cheeky gowl – with his gammy Indian ink tattoo of 'The Saint' on his arm and his little leather sporran – to drive your bumper car and crash into the best-looking women in the other cars on your 20p.

Part of growing up, he explained, was knowing when it was time to steer your own bumper and tell this fella to fuck off back to his little booth and his packet of 10 Major. In holidays as in life as in bumper cars. That was where we were at now. We had outgrown the spins to Beal and Ballybunion; it was time for us to go to Kilkee and stay there for a week. That was how he felt, and she might as well know that he was talking for all the kids.

She told him that she was willing to bet that there wasn't a funfair attendant in Ireland, tattooed or not, that would talk to his own mother in such a foul-mouthed fashion but that it was her own fault for being too easy on him and not giving him the crack across the backside that he should have been getting on the hour, every hour, since she came out of the hospital the first day with him. But she would think about it. And she did think about it. And the upshot of that was that we took a house in Kilkee for a fortnight.

We took the only house we could get, but it coincidentally hit exactly where we would have wanted to end up on the Limerick social and sporting map which was shrunk and superimposed on Kilkee for the three months of summer. The West End of the horseshoe-shaped bay was for the wealthy Ennis Road bourgeoise who owned their houses and supported Old Crescent and Bohemians rugby clubs. The East End was where the Limerick working class rented or traipsed up from their caravans to swim and dream about their beloved Young Munster kicking the fucking heads off those who they could just make out over on the posh side of the beach if they squinted hard – which, by happy coincidence, was their favourite way of looking at anything.

In the middle between those two – the East End ones who ate tripe and the West End ones who used tripe as an adjective to describe anything to do with the east end ones – were the two buffer clubs: Shannon who looked more east, and Garryowen who faced west. We were just to the west of the middle of the seafront where our club allegiance and bank balance could be gauged, but nevertheless outside the two camps staring balefully across the bay at each other, not waving but frowning.

A summer truce was generally observed while all lived, loved, and lushed in the shadow of the colossus who bestrode the bay and the atmosphere every bit as impressively as the wonder that had once stood in Rhodes. Everywhere we went in Kilkee, everywhere we walked, every wall or cliff, every roof, turret, or tuft that was anywhere adjacent to the sea, Richard Harris had jumped off. In the same way that every ancient boat entering Rhodes must have had an awe-inspiring view upwards of a colossal undercarriage, it seemed as if there must have been a decade where every time anyone looked up from their paper or cup of tea, Dickie Harris's tackle was flying over their head.

He was alleged to have lepped off one cliff called the Diamond Rocks and his must have been, if they weren't reduced to powder by the impact from that height. While kids ooohhed and aaahed about the heights and danger of what he was jumping off, murmured conversations and speculative whispers addressed what he was jumping on in his mansion on the way out to the Pollocks. His appetite for women and 'the other thing' was noted with that intoxicatingly hypocritical 'admoniration' that was reserved in a nudging way for open display of male sexual appetite. Walking past his house on the way out for a swim, groups of young fellas would invent lists of the starlets and actresses who they 'knew for a fact' had been entertained within and seen Dicky's jumps from the most interesting angle. But looks were not a prerequisite to meeting the stallion urges of the man called horse.

'He'd ride a warm loaf,' was how an older lad from Janesboro alarmingly put it, only to be bettered by his pal in what is still the most striking visual proposition I think I've ever heard… 'He'd get up on himself, if he could get round quick enough'.

My green narcissus was in full bloom and the only thing I thought Dicky should be getting up on was the scaffold reserved for traitors. I was indignant and mortified that one of our own could have played Cromwell in a movie and, moreover, played our tormenter as a principled if boring farmer with cool hair – Benjy Riordan with dialogue by Voltaire and hair by Vidal Sassoon. Through the cool lad with the skateboard, pretty sister and uncle with expanding coin purse, I met Dicky's French niece who was the same age as us and must have been taken aback to be asked, tout à coup, whether she was embarrassed by her uncle's flattering portrayal of this torturer and mass-murderer? When the poor girl reasonably explained that she was not responsible for her uncle, much less the history of Ireland in the 17th century, I waved all that away and told her that she might understand the offence better if she was to imagine Brigette Bardot wanting to play Eva Braun.

When I think now of her confused face looking back at the prissy, pimply, and self-righteous boy-me, I want to climb up to the highest and most dangerous cliff that Dicky ever jumped from and fall forward with my eyes as closed as my fucking brain was then.

When I wasn't judging French teenage girls for being deficient in Irish cultural sensitivity, I did what everyone else in Kilkee seemed to do: try to work out where you were meant to be swimming and when. The whole place revolved around a swimming schedule and map of daunting complexity only divinable by a priestly caste of old codgers who wore the holy vestments of golf club pringle jumpers over polyester polo-necks. Those that cite Angkor Wat or Stonehenge as wondrous monumental calendars at which it's possible to establish seasons or celestial cycles should be directed to Burn's or Newfie, where attendance at decrepit sheds that smelled of piss could be used to tell exact GMT.

If it was 11.47am then you should be at the First Pollock and wearing togs; if it was 1.10pm then you had to be at Burn's naked; at 3.45pm back over to the pier with togs; 6.15pm trek out to the Third Pollock, togs optional; 8pm Bollock one in Second Pollock and the other bollock in Pollock Three. I think I had (have?) dyscalculia or, as Brother O'Halloran put it, the numeracy competence of a doorknob, and I quickly gave up trying to work out the itinerary and times.

Once freed of that, I began to revel in my outsider status: cheerfully walking miles and whistling my way through the bemused crowds coming against me as they hurried onwards to the mandated location for the next timetabled dip: 'You're going the wrong way, you gowl'.

In fairness to me, and young and snotty as I was, I wasn't ever the kind of kid who was going to be embarrassed about not knowing when the tides were turning or were in or out. If I rambled out to swim in a rock pool only to discover that the tide was fully in and the pool was now 40 fathoms under, then I just swam in whatever water was there. I didn't get the whole trainspotting thing about the best places to swim at certain times; they were probably right, but really, so what?

One thing that I was embarrassed by and about which I made a stand (unfortunate phrase) was the swimming togs that I had been expected to wear. I can't remember if my mother knitted them or just bought the material on one of her camp-overs in Limerick's fabric shops. I can remember however that they were made of scrotum-sculpting fine purple wool that shrink-wrapped itself to every protuberance and wrinkle. You'd have been arrested for public indecency wearing these togs on Fire Island, let alone West Clare. If my pal had been wearing these togs, we'd have no need to ask him whether he was circumcised. He, needless to say, had proper spandex Speedos of the type, stretch and silhouette that left his groin as publicly tidy and harmless as Barbie's Ken.

I told Lady Fecky flat out that I wanted some kind of togs that would themselves flat out any and all embarrassing bulges and shapes. That I was nearly a man now and she should be ashamed of sending me out in front of the whole of Limerick in crocheted togs that were less swimming costume than they were a plaster of Paris model of my undercarriage.

She told me I was imagining things; that no-one gave a tuppeny damn about my togs 'or anything in them' and that she'd decide when I needed new togs. But I'd new shop-bought togs the very next day and Seani's swimming togs – a draw-stringed, high-waisted knitted colander with holes so big it was impossible to work out which ones your legs went through – were also decommissioned and both pairs put out to pasture as dusters.

And it didn't stop at traditional woollen togs; everywhere you looked, long-cherished beliefs, ideals and national icons suddenly found themselves having to defend their previously unquestionable status. Not all were able to survive the interrogation. Chef Salad Cream – for many the very taste of the Irish summer and a staple of the 'Cold Tay' – disappeared so completely after a one-sided smear-off with mayonnaise that just days later you'd forgotten it had ever existed. The bronze-to-iron progression from tinned vegetable salad to edible coleslaw was also underway and developing slowly and fitfully, mostly due to a national wariness of any method of consuming cabbage that deviated from our own tried and trusted three hours of boiling with bacon in the big pot that ideally – as an added probiotic precaution – should also have been used to boil nappies.

The two brands that had struggled for Ireland's soul in a cheesy version of Fine Gael and Fianna Fail's duel-to-the-death, Three Counties and Calvita, were both now elbowed aside as brash newcomers like Cheddar and EasiSingles took centrestage and hours of our time as Paddy's sausage fingers fumbled and pawed at the cellophane wrapping trying to get it open. The moulded rubber that you bit into when you eventually lost patience and sawed your way in with the bread knife was the same material we now wore on our feet as traditional sandals gave way to 'tackies': Jurassic-era airtight trainer shoes that after a single usage was the only thing that a foreigner sniffing the Irish air would have identified as cheese.

It still paid to know your sandals; what you were looking at and what they signified.

In the classic folk tale tradition of not knowing who the dark stranger you're playing cards with is, until – bending under the table to pick up the dropped card – you see the Devil's cloven hoof, it was while I was kneeling down to tie the laces on my airtight rubber tackies that I noticed the sandals being worn by the man queueing at the till of the shop.

Please. No. Struggling to conceal the rising panic, I straightened up, very slowly and discreetly stood back out of his notice to look properly, hoping against hope that what I suspected was not the case.

Fuck. Me.

There was no doubt about it. There was only one group that wore sandals that way. Since the legions last strode forth, only one group could imbue open-toed footwear with so much menace. And they were doing it for Rome, as well. Christian Brothers' sandals were their symbol, the object in which their authority vested. This fella was one. The more I looked the more certain I became. These weren't flimsy summer sandals; these were year-round, quartermaster-issue that pounded the yards, corridors and dreams of Sexton Street, or North Mon or Synge Street or Westland Row, or wherever he was garrisoned. If I'd any doubt about the actual footwear, it was dispelled when I took in the grey heavy hobnailed socks he was wearing.

Oh, he was one, no fucking doubt. In sock signa.

Some panicked enquiries brought confirmation. There was indeed a guest house at which contingents of Brothers stayed but there was no possibility of meeting one of 'ours'. Their dark Satanic majesty depended on only being encountered in situ, in their realm, in their reality. Our teacher brothers were no more interested in seeing us out of season and in civvies than we were in seeing them. To preclude that possibility, the Limerick ones were sent to Tramore, while the Clonmel and Waterford chapters went the other way.

Fears assuaged, I was able to relax and embarked on an every-waking-minute residency of the town's four amusement arcades. It was all as exciting and glamorous as Caesars Palace with our little brat-pack working all the angles all the time to get one over on The House. Staging fights that had one of the combatants hurled into the Penny-nudger at the exact spot most likely to tip the coin-overhang. Scanning the primitive video games for unused credit. Taking turns to monitor the rows of slot machines and identify and play the ones due to pay-out on exactingly estimated timing cycles. Checking automatically behind every 'Coin Return' flap; finger-searching the cavities as quickly as the prison guards were doing in Folsom where Johnny Cash got the blues that he was constantly singing about on the arcade's jukebox.

Being at that time, a several-times daily one-armed bandit myself, I had developed superhuman wrist speed and strength and just the slightest adaptation of technique made me a champion hustler at table soccer. If I felt any lessening of my Olympic gymnast levels of carpal bone speed and strength, I merely hopped into the cinema next door where a close study of Barbara Windsor Bristol Cities in that night's 'Carry On' movie magically restored competition levels of wrist flexibility and grip. When it all became too much and I needed a little mental nap, I might amble down and sit in on a few cards of Pongo – a kind of Remedial Level Bingo for those of us who struggled with numbers. All of life's lessons were there for anyone with two coins to spend, two eyes to see, some time to kill and a brain to fill. It was brilliant and just naturally became the formative experience that formed – and still informs – my idea of what I want to do on the perfect holiday.

AND IT WAS all holidays from then on, asking out loud if anyone wanted to go for a spin was as naff and laughable as asking whether anyone fancied some salad cream or Angel's Delight.

Then just the other day – years and years and years later – I was having coffee and overheard a young one asking her pals whether anyone wanted to go for a spin. They went off with their gym bags and energy, and back I went to the Vauxhall Viva and lost an hour thinking about the concept of spins, if you can believa'.

On the face of it, 'her' going for a spin and 'my' going for a spin are obviously completely different activities; it's scarcely possible to imagine two more differing understandings of the same word, the same verb.

But then, you think about it a little and you compare that now historical understanding of spin – a motorised dander – with the contemporary understanding of spin where that means a group, a class, of people sweating profusely, pedalling furiously on immobile exercise bikes.

Is there not the same repudiation of the idea of destination; the exact same focus on the 'going' – whether motoring or pedalling – as an end-in-itself? The same concession that movement need not be 'to' or 'from' but is valid as a state of being.

There's even the same underlying religious logic that reward must be 'earned': that the right to be able to close the zip on your trousers has to be earned by pedalling for an hour while sitting on an upturned ice-skate. In the same way as the right to eat an ice cream cone has to be earned by spending hours driving across whole counties to buy something that was for sale at the end of your road, and then running the real risk of your first lick dislodging it into your crotch if the incompetent Mr Whippy operator had carelessly filled the cone at an acute angle.

These two meanings of 'going for a spin' would appear to be radically different but are, essentially, the same. They appear as different; they seem to name two different actions. But one minute's reflection tells you that the distinction we make between wasting your time pedalling furiously to go nowhere and driving nowhere to waste your time is arbitrary and specious. They can protest all they like but it seems obvious to me that 'old' spin and 'new' spin are actually one and the same.

The 'new' meaning of spin is the 'old' meaning of spin after a fairly intensive weekend in a discreet clinic with a licence-revoked surgical director, a shitload of anaesthetic, tiger glands and rejuvenating prostate massage by Carola.

The new 'Who wants to go for a spin?' is the old 'Who wants to go for a spin?' but with its arse fat injected into its pectorals and Wayne Rooney's hair on its Micky Rooney head. It's the same deal and comes from the same place as it ever did. It goes to the same place as well: nowhere at all. Or, as Val Doonican used to sing.

No particular place to go.

The Devil has all the Best Tunes

The playlist to accompany *The Devil Wears Farah* will be available on YouTube as soon as we can get some kid to upload it, or 'log on', or do whatever they can do in a minute that would take the likes of you and me two hours that we don't have anymore, where we're staring at the screen as baffled as a goat looking at lightning.

They're Changing Guard at Buckingham Palace by A.A. Milne, sung by Max Bygraves

Two Little Boys by Theodore Morse, sung by Rolf Harris

Is Mise An Tiarna by C. O'Treasaigh (music) and S. O'Cearbhaill (lyrics), sung by Liam Devally, Aedin Ni Choileain and The Young Lindsay Singers

Forty Shades of Green by Johnny Cash

Moon River by Henry Mancini (music) and Johnny Mercer (lyrics), sung by Audrey Hepburn

O'Donnell Abu lyrics by Michael Joseph McCann to traditional air, performed by the RTÉ Concert Orchestra

The Age of Aquarius by Galt MacDermott (music) and James Rado & Gerome Ragni (lyrics), sung by The 5th Dimension

Adeste Fideles by unknown

Wig-Wam Bam by Nicky Chinn and Mike Chapman, sung by Sweet

Have Reindeer, Will Travel by Jerry Livingston and Paul Francis Webster, sung by Johnny Mathis

Have Yourself A Merry Little Christmas by Hugh Martin and Ralph Blane, sung by Johnny Mathis

On the Street where You Live by Frederick Loewe (music) and Alan Jay Lerner (lyrics), sung by Bill Shirley

Ever Loving Adelaide by Frank Loesser, sung by Frank Sinatra

Meet Me in St Louis by Kerry Mills, Arthur B. Sterling, and Conrad Salinger, sung by Judy Garland

I'm in Love with a Wonderful Guy by Richard Rodgers (music) and Oscar Hammerstein (lyrics), sung by Mitzi Gaynor

Oklahoma by Richard Rodgers (music) and Oscar Hammerstein (lyrics), sung by Gordon McRae

Dublin Can Be Heaven by Leo Maguire, sung by Maureen Potter

Sean South by Sean Costelloe, sung by The Wolfe Tones

Brasil! by Ary Barroso

Theme from The Magnificent Seven by Elmer Bernstein

Warm by Sid Jacobson (music) and Jimmy Krondes (lyrics), sung by Johnny Mathis

Chances Are by Robert Allen (music) and Al Stillman (lyrics), sung by Johnny Mathis

The Devil has all the Best Tunes

Baby, Baby, Baby by Jerry Livingston (music) and Mack David (lyrics), sung by Johnny Mathis

Laughing Irish Eyes by Sam H. Stept (music) and Sidney D. Mitchell (lyrics), sung by Arthur Tracy

Did Your Mother Come From Ireland? by Michael Carr and Jimmy Kennedy, sung by Arthur Tracy

It's a Sin to Tell a Lie by Billy Mayhew, sung by Arthur Tracy

It's My Mother's Birthday Today by Tommie Connor and Edward Lisbona, sung by Arthur Tracy

To Mother, With Love by Watson, Denby, Lynton, sung by Arthur Tracy

Gypsy Fiddles by Arthur Tracy and Victor Young, sung by Arthur Tracy

Dane, Gypsy, Dance by Tolchard Evans (music) and Stanley Damerell (music), sung by Arthur Tracy

In a Little Gypsy Tea Room by Joe Burke and Edgar Leslie, sung by Arthur Tracy

Indian Love Song by Robert Friml and Herbert Stothart (music) and Otto Harbach and Oscar Hammerstein (lyrics), sung by Nelson Eddy and Jeanette MacDonald

Hear My Song by Othmar Klose and Rudolf Lukesch, sung by Josef Locke

There is an Isle, Scottish poem put to music by Anna Maria Lynch

When the Red, Red Robin (Comes Bob, Bob, Bobbin' Along) by Harry Woods, sung by Bing Crosby

The Palatine's Daughter, traditional, performed by the RTÉ Concert Orchestra

You Should Be Dancing by the Bee Gees

Speedy's Coming by Rudolph Schenker and Klaus Meine, sung by Scorpions

Thank You, Elvis, medley, sung by Brendan Bowyer

The Hucklebuck by Andy Gibson (music) and Roy Alfred (lyrics), sung by Brendan Bowyer and The Royal Showband

Harvest Supper by Trevor Duncan

Old Shep by Red Foley (music) and Arthur Willis (lyrics), sung by Elvis Presley

Love Me by Mike Stoller (music) and Jerry Lieber (lyrics), sung by Elvis Presley

Clare to the Front, traditional, sung by Michael 'Straighty' Flanagan

Banks of the Sullane, traditional, sung by Ollie Conway

Wooden Heart by Fred Wise, Ben Weisman, Kay Twomey and Bert Kaempfert, sung by Elvis Presley

Spancil Hill, traditional, sung by Johnny McEvoy

Purely by Coincidence by David Parton, sung by Top Of The Pops

The Devil has all the Best Tunes

The Masquerade is Over by Elias Wrubel and Herbert Magidson, sung by Arthur Tracy

The Maid Behind the Bar, traditional, performed by The Dubliners

The Desert Song (Ho, We Sing As We Are Riding) by Sigmund Romberg (music) and Oscar Hammerstein, Otto Harbach and Frank Mandel (lyrics), sung by Mario Lanza

Nellie Kelly, I Love You by George M. Cohan, sung by Judy Garland

Cockeyed Optimist by Richard Rodgers (music) and Oscar Hammerstein (lyrics), sung by Mitzi Gaynor

It Might as well be Spring by Richard Rodgers (music) and Oscar Hammerstein (lyrics), sung by Louanne Hogan

If I Loved You by Richard Rodgers (music) and Oscar Hammerstein (lyrics), sung by Gordon McRae and Shirley Jones

Wouldn't It Be Loverly by Frederick Loewe (music) and Alan Jay Lerner (lyrics), sung by Marni Nixon

Just Blew in from The Windy City by Sammy Fain (music) and Paul Francis Webster (lyrics), sung by Doris Day

The Black Hills of Dakota by Sammy Fain (music) and Paul Francis Webster (lyrics), sung by Doris Day

Climb Ev'ry Mountain by Richard Rodgers (music) and Oscar Hammerstein (lyrics), sung by Margery MacKay

Happy Talk by Richard Rodgers (music) and Oscar Hammerstein (lyrics), sung by Juanita Hall

I Can't Say No by Richard Rodgers (music) and Oscar Hammerstein (lyrics), sung by Gloria Grahame

Goodbye, My Love, Goodbye by Leo Leandros and Klaus Munro, sung by Demis Roussos

Forever and Ever by Alec R. Costandinos and Stélios Vlavianós, sung by Demis Roussos

My Friend The Wind by Alec R. Constandinos and Stélios Vlavianós, sung by Demis Roussos

The White Rose of Athens by Manos Hadjidokis (music) and Hans Bradtke and Nana Mouskouri (lyrics), sung by Nana Mouskouri

Mammy's Tears by Spanner Macken, sung by Buckaroo O'Brien

Mammy's Last Words by Amby Lynch (music) and Butch Kennedy (lyrics), sung by Texas Tim Twomey and Waggon Train

A Mother's Love is a Blessing by T. P. Keenan, sung by Jim McElwainey and The Mighty Mowers

The Only Time that Mammy Touched Satin (Was in Her Coffin) by Nellie O'Neill, sung by Mike Fenton and Fiesta

Lovely Leitrim by Phil Fitzpatrick, sung by Larry Cunningham

Take Me Back to Termonfeckin (And for God's Sake Leave Me There) by Mike Bowen, sung by Patty O'Donnell and The Shiny Scaffold Showband

The Devil has all the Best Tunes

I'm Boilin' to See Boyle by Ignatius Dolan, sung by Seamus O'Toole and the Six Dicks Showband

The Galway Shawl, traditional, sung by Dermot O'Brien

The Shovel that Dug Dulwich (Is Digging Mammy's Grave) by Eoin Reeves, sung by Ger Downes and Galtymore

Whole Lotta Love by Led Zeppelin and Willie Dixon

My Coo Ca Choo by Peter Shelley, sung by Alvin Stardust

Welcome Back My Friends to the Show That Never Ends - Ladies and Gentlemen by Emerson, Lake & Palmer

Love will Tear Us Apart by Joy Division

If I Can't Have You by the Bee Gees, sung by Yvonne Elliman

Emerald by Thin Lizzy

Jailbreak by Phil Lynott, sung by Thin Lizzy

Long Train Runnin by Tom Johnston, sung by The Doobie Brothers

Sara by Stevie Nicks, sung by Fleetwood Mac

The Lamb Lies Down on Broadway by Tony Banks and Peter Gabriel, sung by Genesis

Counting Out Time by Peter Gabriel, sung by Genesis

Pictures at an Exhibition by Modest Mussorgsky, adapted by Emerson, Lake & Palmer

Sweet Leaf by Black Sabbath

R. U. Ready 2 Rock by Sandy Pearlman and Albert Bouchard, sung by Blue Öyster Cult

Cat Scratch Fever by Ted Nugent

Back in the Saddle by Steve Tyler and Joe Perry, sung by Aerosmith

Live in Los Angeles by Budgie

In the Summertime by Ray Dorset, sung by Mungo Jerry

Lola by Ray Davies, sung by The Kinks

Up-Up and Away by Jimmy Webb, sung by The 5th Dimension

No Particular Place to Go By Chuck Berry

Folsom Prison Blues by Johnny Cash

~HYPNOSIS~
MIND OVER PLATTER

~HYPNOSIS~
MIND OVER PLATTER

By

DONALD J. MANNARINO, M.A.

Nationally Certified Clinical Hypnotherapist

Creator of the nationally popular weight loss program

THINK&LOSE

NOW YOU CAN AND YOU WILL LOSE WEIGHT FASTER AND EASIER THAN EVER BEFORE BY FINALLY CHANGING THE WAY YOU THINK ABOUT FOOD!

iUniverse, Inc.

New York Bloomington

Mind over Platter
The Nationally Popular Self-Hypnotic Weight Loss Program—Think & Lose

iUniverse books may be ordered through booksellers or by contacting:

iUniverse
1663 Liberty Drive
Bloomington, IN 47403
www.iuniverse.com
1-800-Authors (1-800-288-4677)

ISBN: 978-1-4401-3843-0 (pbk)
ISBN: 978-1-4401-3841-6 (dj)
ISBN: 978-1-4401-3842-3 (ebk)

Printed in the United States of America

iUniverse rev. date: 5/12/2009

TABLE OF CONTENTS

DEDICATION

To an incredibly supportive, loving & compassionate spiritual guide ~ my wife - Grace.

For Nicco & Tessa, who possess the power to keep their father based in reality with their unconditional love – support & *humor*!

ACKNOWLEDGEMENTS

I would like to extend my sincere gratitude to Larry McAllister of The American Lung Association and Jack Smollinger of The American Heart Association for their vision and trust in my skills and for providing me with the incomparable experience to personally hypnotize thousands of individuals for smoking cessation & weight loss under the umbrella of their respective Associations.

I am indebted to the numerous Hospitals & Corporations that have graciously invited me to personally hypnotize their employees.

A partial list of Hospitals that have presented Don's Hypnosis Seminars:

Good Samaritan Hospital Ashland
Bellevue Hospital
Wood County Health Department
Mercer County Hospital Coldwater
Defiance Regional Medical Center
Fostoria Community
Fremont Memorial Hospital
Hardin Memorial Hospital Kenton
Lima Memorial Hospital
Mansfield General Hospital
Marion Health Center
St. Luke's Hospital Maumee
Morrow County Hospital Mt. Gilead
Fisher Titus Hospital Norwalk

St. Charles Hospital Oregon
Magruder Hospital Port Clinton
St. Mary's Hospital
Firelands Regional Medical Sandusky
Flower Hospital Sylvania
Mercy Hospital Tiffin
St. Anne Hospital Toledo
Toledo Hospital
Wyandot Memorial Hospital
Van Wert Hospital
Fulton County Health Center
O'bleness memorial Athens
SE Regional Medical Center Cambridge
Berger hospital Circleville
Doctors Hospital Nelsonville
Muskingham Hospital Zanesville
Licking Memorial hospital Newark
Akron Children's hospital
Mercy medical Center Canton
Marymount Hospital
Hillcrest Hospital
Robinson memorial Ravenna
Geauga Hospital
St. John's West Shore Hospital
St. Elizabeth's Hospital Youngstown
St. Joes Hospital Warren
Lake County West Hospital
Drake Medical Center Cincinnati
United Way Batavia
Georgetown Hospital
West union Hospital
Hillsboro Hospital
DePaul Hospital
Clinton Hospital Wilmington
Community Hospital Springfield
Greene City Health Dept. Xenia

A partial list of Health Associations that have presented Don's Hypnosis Seminars

American Lung Association of Ohio
American Lung Association of Michigan

American Lung Association of Indiana
American Heart Association of Cleveland
American Heart Association of Youngstown
American Heart Association of Columbus
American Heart Association of Canton

***A partial list of Corporations that have presented Don's Hypnosis Seminars*:**

Ford Motor Corporation
Delphi
Chrysler Corp.
Goodyear
Crown Battery
GM Powertrain
GEM Corp.
PPG
L.E. Berry Co.
Coca-Cola
General Mills
Smythe-Cramer
Smead Corp.
Superior Clay
McDonald-Hopkins
Hobart Corp.
Ohio Casualty
Cooper farms
V & M Star
Bosch-Rex Roth
J & L Steel
Lowe's Corp.
Little Tykes
H.C. Starck Medical
O'Cedar Brand
International Paper
ITT Industries
Dynatech
Forest City Enterprises

FORWARD

According to the Center for Disease Control, (CDC), the prevalence of obesity among adults aged 20–74 years increased from 15.0% to 32.9% over the last 20 years. This means 1 out of every three Americans are considered to be obese! Further, 66%, or 2 out of 3 are deemed to be overweight!

The CDC estimated 142,000,000 U.S. adults (age 20 and older) are overweight - about 73,000,000 males, 69,000,000 females. This represents about 66.0 percent of the adult population. Of these, *67.3 million are obese!*

A 40-year-old overweight male will lose 3.1 years of life - one who is obese will lose 5.8 years!

A 40-year-old overweight female will lose 3.3 years of life - one who is obese will lose 7.1 years!

More than 9 million children and adolescent ages 6–19 are considered overweight. Overweight adolescents have a 70 percent chance of becoming overweight adults. This increases to 80 percent if one or both parents are overweight or obese.

The World Health organization (WHO) estimates that by 2015, the number of overweight people worldwide will increase to 2.3 billion, and more than 700 million will be obese. Currently, at least 20 million children worldwide under age 5 are overweight!

According to the American heart Association the average adult woman weighs in at a staggering 163! Perhaps the most shocking statistics underscoring obesity in the United States is that 400,000 Americans (mostly men) fall into a super-massive 400 plus category.

According to the American Heart Association obesity is a key changeable risk factor for preventing cardiovascular disease. Being overweight increases the potential for high cholesterol, high blood pressure and type 2 diabetes, which are each major risk factors for other serious health problems. Recent research suggests that obesity shortens a person's lifespan by four to nine months, and if childhood obesity continues to increase, it could cut two to five years from the average individual's lifespan. This could cause the current generation of children to become the first in United States history to live shorter lives than their parents. Overweight and obesity by middle age are directly linked. The direct cost of overweight and obesity is $92 billion and indirect cost is $40 billion.

<u>WHY MY THINK & LOSE HYPNOSIS PROGRAM:</u> because it is imperative that Americans learn how to condition the *<u>mind</u>* to make healthier food choices, motivate the *<u>mind</u>* to eat less and

strengthen the resolve of the *mind* to become more physically active. The choices individuals make about what they eat and their activity level have an undeniable role in the rise of overweight and obesity.

According to the American Heart Association, **the causes of being overweight and/or obese is simply too much of the wrong foods! Increased calorie consumption is clearly the problem. In addition, many of our food choices are not meeting our individual nutritional needs. This was one of the most important aspects when formulating my hypnosis weight loss suggestions for the seminars I conducted for the American Heart Association 1978–1986 and The American Lung Association 1986-2005.**

A recent U.S. Surgeon General report affirmed that obesity is responsible for 300,000 deaths every year. These overwhelming research statistics reveal an alarming overweight and obesity trend, the need for personal action. In the center of the magnitude of information and research available on the overweight and obesity epidemic, statistics are exceptionally easy to find. The most widely circulated CDC research statistic on American obesity indicates that 63% of Americans are overweight and more than 25% have been declared obese. Concerning overweight and obesity in kids the most riveting statistic shows that childhood obesity has more than tripled over the past 20 years.

For the millions of men, women and children who experience the daily frustrations and the stressful impact to their self- confidence and self-

esteem because of their body weight – consider this: I can show you how you can lose weight faster and easier than ever before. I can teach you, through the powerful relaxation of clinical hypnosis how you can and will finally change your thoughts so that you can and you will change your destiny.

It seems that every day the media is reminding us of the difficulty and unhealthiness of being overweight. A recent article in The Cleveland Plain Dealer, August 28, 2007: "two-thirds of Americans are overweight or obese." We're constantly reminded that we are a flabby nation. That we eat way too much and of course we eat all the wrong foods. That we do not exercise and being overweight is a major contributor to heart diseases, diabetes, stroke and other diseases and various types of health related maladies.

As a nation, we have set in motion the continuation of overeating and obesity on to our children. We are all aware of the depression and stress being overweight generates both physically and emotionally. The time has come for all of us to recognize the need to change the way we think about food, the choices we choose to make and the quantity of the foods we are choosing to eat. Stimulating one's mind and body to consider exercise in the philosophy that any movement above zero is good movement.

With this assertion in mind and heart I present to you my time tested - positive weight loss hypnosis program appropriately titled Think & Lose: it is time to set your mind in motion to become and remain thin and slim again. You used

to be – you're the one who changed your eating thoughts and I am the one who can teach you how to change those thoughts back to greater self-control again!

Don Mannarino

MIND CONTROL & TRANSFORMATION

Donald J. Mannarino, M.A.

It has always been said that everyone has a story – this is mine!

It started in junior high for me when I realized I was different. I was not as tall, attractive, smart or popular as so many of my school mates. Many of you know all too well the feeling of isolation and the thoughts of wishing to be better looking and popular, I knew I did.

The pain and loneliness I felt at that time in my life could not of course be expressed verbally because I simply did not know how to talk about my feelings or who to talk about them to. I ended up internalizing these negative self-defeating thoughts and became an angry teenager. I found myself drawn to other angry teenagers and discovered a common bond of similarity. Like attracts like!

This confusion and anger set the groundwork and framework of my high school years! When I was alone I would wish and pray to God that I

could feel different about myself but wishing and hoping only seemed to make my feelings of self-esteem diminish more for it constantly reinforced the reality of what I looked like and unless a miracle happened I was forever to be this ugly, unpopular, feared, angry kid.

My high school years were wrought with sadness and anger. Sure I had some friends but they were all intimidated by me. Some people internalize their anger and become depressed I on the other hand externalized it. I only succeeded in alienating what few friends I had until there was only one person, believe it or not a girl, who actually liked me. Her parents didn't what a surprise, I worked hard at cultivating a bad reputation and now I was being recognized, negatively for it!

I was your classic Italian street greaser punk complete with Brylcreem in my long wavy slick-black hair - Lucky Strike non filter cigarette on my lips, the legendary black leather ¾ length jacket, black pointed spit-shined shoes complete with wing-tip, white pencil around the stitching and cleats (toe & heel), Sansabelt pants (worn high above the waist of course) and tight knit Ban Lon shirts to show off – you guessed it my biceps - oh and yea fists of fury and a temper to match – and I even drove a 1956 Chevy Belair!

Needless to say I succeeded in making more enemies, alienating those that thought they wanted to be my friend and it only served to further distance me from others. I knew what I was doing was wrong and I wanted to change but I just did not know how. I thought I was the one who was always right and everyone else was wrong. Later

in life, as I reflected on those years, I realized that when I hurt inside I would lash out and only hurt others In turn.

In high school I had two things going for me I could fight and I could dance. Almost certainly because at dances is where the best fights would be! Fast forward to 1970 all hell is breaking loose at the Kent State campus, Vietnam is raging, SDS is growing, fashions have become long hair and flowery clothes, jargon changed – and the age of moving from greasers to collegian to mod - and eventually to hippie seemed to happen overnight.

So there I was the world is changing around me and I still pondered why did I have to be so ugly... why didn't girls like me...why was it cool that other boys feared me...why? The harder I tried to be different the more I stayed the same. I had created the persona that I myself could not break out of. I had set up my life so that others expected me to behave in certain ways and I felt obligated to fulfill their expectations and then some.

Through those years I still had one positive anchor in the form of a girlfriend. Even though we could not see each other and had to sneak around for almost 3 years she taught me, without ever knowing it, the true meaning of compassion and understanding. I learned the importance of recognizing the good potential in others even though the person himself could not see or feel it.

Throughout all this turmoil, each and every night as I went to sleep, I began to repeat in my mind the same prayer thought..."Dear God please help me to become handsome, healthy, wealthy and

better looking..." I started going to the Shrine of Our lady of Lourdes with my girl friend and prayed for guidance and direction, but mostly because we could go there and no one else would suspect us to be there and hence no one was around so it became a safe haven for us.

As the years passed my looks started to change, my thoughts changed, my life began to change because all because my philosophy of asking for what I wanted and believing I would achieve it was actually working. I had decided to go to college on my own and discovered as well as implement the innate intelligence I had suppressed for so many years with misdirected anger. I was discovering how to control my destiny. I wanted more. As I had mentioned when I was a kid I was drawn to hypnosis because I thought if I could hypnotize people I could control them and the really get the things I wanted. The whole time I thought about hypnotizing others with that controlling power I was actually beginning to hypnotize my self through the repetition of "my nightly prayer."

I was slowly developing a charisma that others found attractive and positive in nature. It was an incredible awareness to discover that I and I alone possessed the true power to change my thoughts and my destiny. I could control my environment and therefore my own happiness.

For the rest of my life, an even to this very day, each and every night I would tell my mind exactly what I wanted to achieve.

Consistency & repetition are the essential jewels to making your dreams become reality.

I was able to utilize theses same principles when it became important for me to lose weight. I lost 25 pounds in one month by utilizing the concepts of eating less combined with the incredible power of hypnosis.

I believed deeply in my heart and mind and soul that what I thought about and wanted to have and become would in fact become true...after all I had already changed my looks, changed my health (stopped smoking - started exercising), changed my attitude towards education, changed every aspect of my life.

Then along came Grace the love I had longed for my entire life. I met her and the world stopped. I went home and changed my prayer: dear God please bring this woman into my life." Here it is over 24 years later two children Nicco and Tessa loving life and everything and everyone in it.

I want you to know and really believe in the power of your mind. That by making the choice to achieve the goals you truly wish to achieve combined with the power of positive thought with consistency and repetition you can and you will change your destiny.

"I firmly believe, without any doubt whatsoever, that I personally altered my entire physicality, destiny & existence though the knowledge and utilization of the incredible power of thought control. It is my intention to enlighten - educate and encourage all of you to learn how you can and will alter your own life circumstances in a positive manner by the natural power of hypnosis." Don

HOW OUR MIND WORKS

In order to begin to understand the principle of changing your thoughts so that you can and will change your destiny understand this assertion: *nothing happens by chance only by choice!*

The true power center of the brain lies within the subconscious mind. Hypnosis is the most positive and strongest method of reaching and programming the subconscious mind.

Let me briefly explain: essentially our mind works on 3 levels: our conscious mind, subconscious mind & unconscious.

The conscious mind is simply our awareness in everyday life. In Freud's psychoanalytic theory of personality, the conscious mind includes everything that is inside our awareness. This is the aspect of our mental processing that we can think and talk about in a rational way. **The conscious mind** includes everything that we are aware of. This is the feature of our mental processing where we can think and talk about rationally. A part of this includes our accumulated memory which can be retrieved easily at any time and brought into our awareness

On the other hand, the unconscious state of mind simply means that you are asleep and unaware of your surroundings. Sleep is a physical and mental inactive state of mind in which a person becomes relatively unaware of the world around him. In essence, sleep is a partial detachment from the world, where most external stimuli are blocked from the senses.

The subconscious is the true power center of the brain. It is the inner voice so to speak that guides us in our decisions & choices. It is an automatic conditioning process of the mind that thru repetition becomes the way we act, believe, feel, and the choices we make, the control or lack of control over our own life. What the subconscious mind believes to be true becomes true.

The subconscious mind is where the real power of hypnosis has its direct and positive influence for those who truly want to lose weight.

Your subconscious mind is where you control your emotions and behaviors and the best method of reaching your subconscious mind is through the relaxed state of hypnosis. Many websites state that Hypnosis has been approved by the AMA since 1958. The APA has the Division 30 Society of Psychological Hypnosis dedicated to the professional applications of hypnosis.

Over the past 30 years I have specialized in the use of clinical hypnosis for cognitive modification that is, using powerful and positive hypnosis suggestions to change the way a person thinks about food both in choice and quantity. You are what you think and The Think and Lose Weight Loss Program can and will provide you with the

healthy positive suggestions you need to finally once and for all learn to change the way you think about food and ultimately lose the weight you desire.

Most gratifying to me personally has been the wide acceptance of the clinical application of hypnosis. I help people stop smoking, lose weight, manage stress and enhance the quality of their personal lives in many positive ways. I have enjoyed and experienced first hand how the subject and technique of clinical hypnosis has experienced an incredible surge in popularity both in the medical and psychological arenas.

As a clinical hypnotist, I have received numerous questions from individuals that have a variety of concerns and hopes regarding the application of hypnosis for various dilemmas. In the chapter on Wellness Hypnosis Programs I have list of current hypnosis programs I have devoted my practice, research and development to over the past 30 years.

This book is designed to open your mind and heart to the incredible powerful relaxing benefits of clinical hypnosis. How it can and will overcome many stressful situations they many of you are confronted with in your daily life specifically with regard to losing weight and keeping it off.

My book is designed to offer the reader a brief overview of the history of hypnosis, a very practical and easily understood definition of hypnosis, what it actually feels like to be hypnotized and answer the many questions that many of you may have. It is my belief that once you, the reader, fully

understand the true clinical benefits of hypnosis a positive self-directed decision can and will be made regarding its appropriate application to your own personal needs and goals.

Unfortunately, throughout the years hypnosis has generally been shrouded in mystery and entertainment. My book will dispel the myths and misconceptions of hypnosis and give you the reader an interesting and realistic inner view of what the world of hypnosis, when used correctly, can and will help you achieve.

My explanation and life philosophy of hypnosis is defined as: a positive thought centered lifestyle – for you always become what you choose to think. Thru the right application of positive thought (suggestions) you can and you will learn to direct your mind toward the positive application of reaching your weight loss goal.

It is truly amazing what the world of hypnosis, when used properly, can and will achieve for the human condition!

HISTORY OF HYPNOSIS

The modern scientific understanding of hypnosis originated with the pioneering work of the Scottish physician named James Braid (1795-1860). Braid, who coined the term 'hypnotism' published his findings in Neurypnology (1843). Braid's later view that his own expression 'hypnotism' from the Greek word for sleep, was essentially a misnomer and his attempts to substitute the name monoideism (fixation upon a single idea) never really caught on. The medical practice of hypnotherapy has subsequently been approved by the British Medical Association (BMA), in 1892 and followed by the American Medical Association (AMA) in 1958. Three years after the BMA report the American Medical Association (AMA) followed suit by officially approving a two-year study by their Council on Mental Health, led by Dr. M. Ralph Kaufman. In this report, the AMA, like the BMA, recognized hypnotherapy as an orthodox medical treatment.

Early history

Sleep temples

"..And God cast Adam into a 'deep sleep'... King James Bible

Virtually all-ancient civilizations practiced the art of "temple sleep" which was used to induce a sleep like trance for healing.
The earliest findings of hypnosis date back to the Egyptian Sleep Temples. Using the mind and thoughts have been used since ancient times to heal the mind and the body. Meditation, incantations, tribal rituals, ceremonial dances, chanting, Lamaze and Yoga are all associated forms of hypnosis.

Franz Anton Mesmer

Western scientists first became involved in hypnosis around 1770, when Dr. Franz Mesmer (1734-1815), a physician from Austria, started investigating an effect he called "animal magnetism" or "mesmerism" (the latter name still remaining popular today). Anton Mesmer was a physician practicing in France when he came into notoriety regarding his discovery of magnetism. Mesmer based his theory on the magnetism that the universe generated and which he and he alone could gather into a direct healing energy through the use of magnets. By using magnets he would be able to gather the invisible rays of magnetism energy and by the laying or touching of theses magnetized elements he could in fact generate a cure at the point of ouch to the diseased part of the body. In time of course he began to magnetize a wand and would touch his patients accordingly. in further development he believed he could use his hands to effect the same magnetic cure. he also began experimenting with groups at this time more often made up of women. Mesmer would induce what he called a crisis thru the laying on of hands that were magnetized and be able to cure any

disorder. In time it was discovered that magnetism did not exist and the cures were actually a direct result of expectation combined with the patient's imagination that something of a healing nature was actually going on. Of course the prominence of Mesmer's reputation also helped effect this cure as well. Anton Mesmer (mesmerism) was without a doubt the most influential proponent of the art of suggestion. Hypnotism

James Braid

The evolution of Mesmer's ideas and practices led the Scottish neurosurgeon James Braid in 1842 to coin the term, and develop the procedure known as, "hypnosis." Popularly called the "Father of Modern Hypnotism," Braid rejected Mesmer's idea that hypnosis was induced by magnetism, and ascribed the "mesmeric trance" to a physiological process resulting from prolonged attention to a bright moving object or similar object of fixation. He postulated that "protracted ocular fixation" fatigued certain parts of the brain and caused a trance—a "nervous sleep" or, from the Greek, "neuro-hypnosis." Later Braid simplified the name to "hypnosis" (from the Greek *Hypnos*, def. sleep). Finally, realizing that "hypnosis" was *not* a kind of sleep, he sought to change the name to monoideaism (single-idea), but the term "hypnosis" had stuck. Braid tried hypnotism to treat various psychological and physical disorders. He had little success, especially with "organic" (that is, "physical," or non-psychological) conditions. Braid is credited with writing the first book on hypnosis, *Neurypnology* (1843).

Jean-Martin Charcot

The neurologist Jean-Martin Charcot (1825-1893) endorsed hypnotism for the treatment of hysteria. *La méthode numérique* (The numerical method) led to a number of systematic experimental examinations of hypnosis in France, Germany, and Switzerland. The process of post-hypnotic suggestion was first described in this period. Extraordinary improvements in sensory acuity and memory were reported under hypnosis.

American Civil War

Hypnosis was used by field doctors in the American Civil War and was the first extensive medical application of hypnosis. Although hypnosis seemed to be very effective in the field[with the introduction of the hypodermic needle and the general chemical anesthetics of ether in 1846 and chloroform in 1847 to America, it was much easier for the war's medical community to use chemical anesthesia than hypnosis. Other physicians claimed better results, particularly in using hypnosis for pain control. An 1842 report described a painless amputation performed on a hypnotized patient. This was widely dismissed, and there was strong resistance in the medical profession to the idea of hypnosis; but there followed other reports of success.

British Medical Association, 1955

On April 23, 1955, the British Medical Association (BMA) approved the use of hypnosis in the areas of psychoneuroses and hypnoanesthesia in pain management in childbirth and surgery. At this time, the BMA also advised all physicians and medical students to receive fundamental training in hypnosis.

American Medical Association, 1958

In 1958, the American Medical Association approved a report on the medical uses of hypnosis. It encouraged research on hypnosis although pointing out that some aspects of hypnosis are unknown and controversial.

Milton Erickson

(1901-1980) developed many ideas and techniques in hypnosis that were very different from what was commonly practiced. His style, commonly referred to as Ericksonian Hypnosis, has greatly influenced many modern schools of hypnosis.

Clark Hull

By the 1920s, hypnosis became the focus of experimental investigation by psychologists like Clark L. Hull (1884-1952), who demystified hypnosis saying that it was essentially a normal part of human nature (1933). The important factor was the subject's imagination - some people were

more responsive or suggestible than others to hypnosis.

Theodore X. Barber

(1927-2005) Theodore X. Barber , a psychologist who became a leading proponent of hypnosis the power of positive suggestion after his scientific studies concluded that the power of suggestion often worked nearly as well.. In 1969, Dr. Barber published a book, Hypnosis: A Scientific Approach, that helped to place hypnotic phenomena in the mainstream of social psychology. Also in the 1960's, Dr. Barber's research introduced the Barber Suggestibility Scale, a method of evaluating individuals and measuring their responsiveness to a range of suggestions. The hypnotizability scale is still in use today. Dr. Barber developed what became career-long study of hypnosis and was one of the most prolific researchers and publishers of scientific hypnosis data. One of his main contributions to the world of hypnosis is in his discovery of the unnecessary use of the swinging watch and the scientific dismissal of stage hypnosis as pure cooperative entertainment, similar to the popular children's game: Simon Says.

I had the personal privilege of meeting with Dr. Barber in 1978. What he taught me continues to thrive within my own research and application of the true power of the subconscious mind and positive suggestion.

There is great deal of research that convincing supports evidence that certain forms of clinical and cognitive hypnotic procedures are exceptionally

effective in the management alleviation of pain. The practice of cognitive hypnosis can significantly reduce general anxiety, tension and stress. It most certainly can help you re-gain your self-control, self-confidence and self-discipline with regards to weight loss and a wide variety of other personal issues. For a brief synopsis on various applications see the chapter on wellness hypnosis programs.

Around the middle of the 19th century hypnosis readily became a vehicle for showmen. Vaudevillians-charlatans-sideshow-traveling medicine men used to entertain with fraudulent stooges in there copy cat performances. This could very well be why so many individuals associate hypnosis with acting like a chicken. It is pure entertainment.

TRUE SECRETS

Its time to share with you my inner most personal and powerful secret to success and true happiness. There are two very specific persons whose personal philosophies have been, and will continue to be, the guiding light – power and positive force in my daily life. In fact, how I use the strength of my own thought control to succeed. These two incredibly insightful individuals understood without a doubt the power of thought with regard to influencing the universe: James Allen, As a Man Thinketh and Robert S. Clason, The Richest Man in Babylon.

What I have learned about the character and personality of the human condition, including the mastery of my own destiny was derived from these two exceptional men. Although I will discuss their philosophies in general I implore you to read and thoroughly study their concepts well and you will come to know and understand that the authentic secret to the universe lies within your own mind and you were born with the key to unlock that power. Include these two books in your study for life. I have read and studied and most importantly applied their philosophies as if they were my very own for over 35 years. Today, they are without still

the two most important theories regarding my life principles and the choices I make.

Up until now I have only shared them with my wife, son and daughter. For the very first time I will reveal to all of you the real power of self-directed destiny! The future is yours and everything with it and all for the asking. I welcome you to explore their philosophies as we enter the journey to unravel the secrets to weight loss, to help you put the puzzle together, to discover the true rhythm of your own true destiny.

JAMES ALLEN: AS A MAN THINKETH

James Allen (1864-1912) wrote his book for those who are seeking insight, understanding, wisdom and happiness with regard to positive thinking. James Allen believed in the power of thought to change ones destiny.

Here is a direct quote by James Allen:

"They themselves are makers of themselves."

The mind is the master weaver, of the inner garment of character and the outer garment of circumstance. This is so insightful for it tells us that the mind controls it all.

"A man is literally what he thinks."

Your existence, level of success and happiness, even if your bodyweight, did not happen by chance rather as a direct result of the sum of all our own thoughts. Thoughts that you chose and did not happen by chance.

"Every act of a man springs from the hidden seeds of thought."

Becoming overweight did not happen to you by chance rather by your own direct choice. Sadness

and depression become the consequence of the seeds to overeat and snack in excess.

"Man is made or unmade by himself."

In the mind is where you create the thoughts that lift you to success and happiness or the thoughts that destroy you and breed depression. In the mind with Think and Lose you will learn how to create the right thought to finally succeed at losing the weight that you desire.

"Man is the master of thought, the molder of character, and the maker and shaper of condition, environment and destiny."

You and you only determine your destiny. Your personality is the sum of all the choices you have made and continue to make. The world in which you live is also the direct result of your decisions in life. If you truly want to improve your circumstances you must be willing to improve yourself. Although you may not necessarily be able to control your specific circumstances you can however control your thought processes and therefore indirectly control and influence your circumstances.

"He that seeketh findeth; and to him that knocketh it shall be opened."

Once you possess the motivation to lose the weight you desire then you must choose to persevere and be ready to open all the doors that lead to success with consistency and repetition. You are the one who must instigate the changes in your life.

"Man is the master gardener of his mind."

When it comes to losing weight analyze for yourself whether you choose to plant negative

seeds of thought within your mind which can only cultivate weeds and therefore negative emotions. Exercise your right to control your body weight by planting for yourself positive thoughts that will blossom into positive results for you.

"The outer conditions of a persons life will always be found to be harmoniously related to his inner state."

You are not overweight by chance rather by direct choice. This did not just happen to you, you're the one who made the choice to overeat and therefore I one who must change that thought process. If you feel out of control in your thoughts your body weight will most definitely reflect it. Happiness, health and personal growth and prosperity occur as a direct result of living in harmony with your surroundings.

"Good thoughts bear good fruit, bad thoughts bear bad fruit."

The positive affirmations, I can, I will, I am, create for you and insurmountable amount of positive energy and movement towards your personal desire to be thin – slim & healthy. The negative affirmations I can't, I won't, I'm not, create a surge of negative energy and movement away from your desire to be thin and the reinforcement of being overweight and unhealthy. When you can alter your thought process you will radically alter the conditions of your life. To be thin – slim and healthy or not to be thin – slim and healthy – really is the question – isn't it!

"The body is the servant of the mind."

James Allen is very explicit regarding health as you may well imagine he strongly believed, of course, that negative thoughts will be expressed in a negative unhealthy body. If you fear being overweight that fear will manifest itself in the body and you will become overweight. Those who live in fear of contracting a disease will subconsciously bring it on. Unhealthy eating thoughts bring on unhealthy overweight issues. Knowing that your body directly responds to the thoughts you choose to think then choose pure strong healthy thoughts of eating less and choosing foods that are good for you rather than foods that are rich and fattening.

I could go on and on with these parallels of James Allen's philosophies to the premise of losing weight. Let me leave you with this last thought to ponder: diets will not help someone who refuses to change their thought patterns. Hypnosis is the method to do so- thin thoughts breed a clean healthy thin body.

You must have a purpose in your life otherwise your mind becomes cluttered with negative worries generally based in stress and anxiety and the past. Your purpose is to become thin and slim again and you need to put your heart and soul into accomplishing it. Choose to experience successful weight loss and you can and you will. No more doubt or fear of failure rather positive purpose with the determination to do the things you truly want to do for yourself!

The theory to success is plain and simple, all that you achieve or fail to achieve is the direct result of the thoughts you choose to think. It is

time for you to lift your thoughts to a higher level of personal excellence than ever before. Practice my formula of consistency and repetition with positive thoughts and you can and will accomplish anything you desire.

GEORGE S. CLASON: THE RICHEST MAN IN BABYLON

In 1926, George S. Clason wrote the book, The Richest Man in Babylon, as a treatise on the subject of thrift and financial planning as based on ancient Babylonian parables. The focus is to guide the reader towards a path to prosperity and happiness.

George Clason describes succinctly the premise that our actions can be no wiser than our thoughts. According to Clason, preparation is the key to success. You are the one who must make the decision that if you are to achieve your weight loss goal for example time and study are valued traits.

Clason's book will make clear to you the ancient methods of curing a lean purse. More precisely, how to acquire money, how to keep it, and how to use it.

The insight and wisdom presented by Clason with specific regards to his seven cures for a lean

purse, are a must read for all who desire financial stability. Briefly listed here are the seven cures:

1. **Start thy purse to fattening!**
2. **Control thy expenditures!**
3. **Make thy gold multiply!**
4. **Guard thy treasures from loss!**
5. **Make thy dwelling a profitable investment!**
6. **Insure a future income!**
7. **Increase thy ability to earn!**

George Clason's philosophy, A man's wealth is not in the purse he carries. A fat purse quickly empties if there be no golden stream to refill it. To me personally this is the most inspirational proverb I have ever learned. I encourage all of you to take time to read and study this most credible classic.

THE EXPERIENCE OF HYPNOSIS

Calmness of mind is one of the beautiful jewels of wisdom. It is the result of long and patient effort in self-control. James Allen

If you have seen my infomercial, thinkandlose.com, it starts with the premise: "If hypnosis can help you walk over hot coals then it sure can help you to strengthen the minds desire to control the foods you choose to eat and lose the weight that you truly want to lose."

People always ask me what it feels like to be hypnotized-? I tell them it's by far the most soothing-relaxing incredible experiences one can imagine. In fact sometimes the experience of hypnosis is better than sleep itself - and yet, your mind becomes relaxed, focused, and concentrated all at once. It's like when you drive in a car and your listening to the radio, watching traffic, thinking about work, the kids, talking on the cell, and you pull into your driveway yet you have no clue how in fact you got there-yet you were indeed fully wide awake! It's also like when you read a good book and you become so engrossed and concentrated on what you are reading that you become oblivious

to your surroundings, yet sometimes after reading for awhile you actually cannot remember what it was you just read-yet you were indeed fully wide awake! It's also like when and athlete psyches him/her self up to perform to the maximum of their potential, to get in the zone. And is oblivious to pain – yet indeed fully wide awake! It's when a woman has a baby through natural child-birth and practices the rhythm of breathing to diminish pain-yet indeed fully wide awake!

There are many daily forms of hypnosis during which your mind slips into a daydream trance without you realizing it until you 'come out' of the daydream. Hypnosis is focus, concentration & relaxation at its purest. It is a relaxed state of mind that can enable you to reprogram your thoughts and to ultimately enhance your positive behaviors and diminish your negative unwanted behaviors. It is without a doubt the strongest and quickest way to achieve personal growth and development I base this conclusion on the time-tested adage... "what the mind thinks always becomes true..."

The word trance conjures up the illusion that a person is totally unaware of where and what they are doing. Well why is it when you are in a trance behind the wheel of a car your still able to make all the appropriate decisions to drive and get to your destination? Why is it when you are in a trance you are able remember details upon being prompted? Why is it that you can perform at a higher level of excellence when your mind is highly focused and entranced and concentrated? Interesting thought right? The true definition of trance in my experience is the ability to minimize external and sometimes internal distractions.

Hypnosis is a very pleasant medically safe and relaxed state of mind and body. Often time quite better than sleep itself. For instance, many people sleep but they don't relax they wake up still feeling tired and fatigued they just don't rest the mind and body. By the way did you ever go to sleep at night thinking silently what time you must get up in the morning because you have a very important meeting – so you proceed to set your time clock and lo and behold your mind wakes you up 10 minutes before the alarm goes off!

HYPNOSIS INDUCTION

The following is an example of the suggestions I make when beginning the induction of hypnosis for weight loss: "close your eyes and begin to listen to the sound of my voice and the suggestions I give you. Slowly start by taking a nice long slow breath in – fill the lungs to capacity-breathe out slowly...good, once again slow breath in...this time breath is out faster and drop your shoulders, relax your arm, relax your legs begin now to quiet down & settle down...do not rush this we have lots and lots of time...so let us use it wisely...again with me now long slow deeper breath in...hold it...now exhale quickly and drop the whole body like a rag doll...go right back in to your breathing and notice how much easier the air begins to flow down thru the inside length of your lungs...other sounds and thoughts do not matter...time to let other sounds and thought begin to fade out and fade away becoming less and less important...all that is important is the sound of my voice and the relaxed rhythm of your own breathing...time begins to slow down...your breathing slows down...the mind itself begins to slow down...hypnosis already begins to feel better than you thought it would... the time is now to learn the art of self-hypnosis...I want you to think about the muscles in your....

I continue to go thru the entire body relaxing muscles and slowing the breathing...focusing on deep mind/body relaxation...when the mind relaxes the mind becomes receptive...when you are using hypnosis suggestions for weight loss and this is what your focus is then your mind becomes hyper receptive . You will find that you can concentrate deeper and easier on the suggestions I give you:

Obviously, this is a much abbreviated format of one of my most popular inductions of hypnosis. As you may well imagine this becomes an extremely relaxing sensation to your mind and body and medically good and safe for everyone.

THINK & LOSE: OUTLINE

The one thing all of you know for certain is that although you may in fact lose weight while dieting, once the diet comes to an end you end up going right back to your old eating thoughts. Its your mind that got you into this and its your mind that will get you out. I always ask this, what if you could go anywhere you want, eat anything you want, whenever you want, and why ever you want and still lose weight! Well now, you would have the key to the kingdom wouldn't you!

Is the problem when you eat – NO!

Is the problem why you eat – NO!

Is the problem how you eat – NO!

The problem today is the same problem you have always had, it's not when why or how it's the quantity! Always has been and always will be. When you eat too much your body weight goes up right! Conversely, when you eat less your body weight goes down – also right! So if all you need to do is eat less how does something so easy becomes so complicated for you? Why is it , you sit down to eat, you have great intentions, and you

end up eating too fast and subsequently eating too much.

When you eat too much you get mad at yourself, then what you eat because you're mad and angry! Then you get depressed – and what do you do when your depressed – you guessed it you eta some more – then you say oh, well, this diet doesn't work I'll go on another one Monday! Perhaps its only Monday afternoon, chances are you stayed up late on Sunday too eat everything you could get your hands on so you could start your new diet on Monday morning!

Let me ask you this: have you ever gone on a diet Tuesday afternoon? How about Thursday morning? Chances are NO you never have it's always a Monday!

Unless you are on a diet for medical reasons, e.g. diabetic, high blood pressure, cardiovascular reasons etc, NO MORE DIETING! Come on you're a professional when it comes to dieting. You go on a diet you lose the weight the diet ends you go right back to your old eating thoughts! It's the mind – your mind that must change!

Here's a question for all of you: How many of you eat when -

Depressed? Happy?

Alone? With others?

How many of you eat all the time?

Get it! You are not overweight by chance rather by choice your choice. Being overweight did not

just happen to you – you're the one who made the choice to overeat! You started this and now you've forgotten how to change it and control it. Until now!

Think and lose is based on the premise that by changing your thoughts about food you can and you will learn to eat less. By reducing your caloric intake your body weight must go down! After all by eating too much your body weight has gone up – right!

The trick is to eat less and feel content! Fullness, hunger, appetite is not in your stomach it's in your mind – your subconscious mind and always has been. I know where the subconscious mind is, how to reach it and the rhythm to change it.

Desire, motivation, self-honesty are the necessary ingredients for changing your thoughts. Through the power of your own mind your own thoughts you can and you will learn how to eat less make healthier more nutritious choices, eat less and lose the weight that you truly want to lose.

NO DENIAL – NO RESTRICTION & NO MORE TEMPTATION:
YOU SEE IT – YOU WANT IT – IT'S YOURS!

That sounds too good to be true doesn't it. Well then think about this: thru the suggestions I give you, you will finally have the freedom to go any where you want and eat anything you want – no denial no restriction, you can no longer cheat – no guilt – you see it its yours!

Now take a moment and think about this: eating anything you want and still losing the weight you desire – sound amazing! ***Keep reading...***

During hypnosis I will give you positive suggestions to lose your urge, craving and desire and addiction to sugars, sweets, candy, pastry pop, salty snacks, etc. I will then give your mind the positive suggestions to start choosing the foods that are good and nutritious for you rather than the foods that were rich and fattening an your weight will fall off!

I want to teach you how to utilize the incredible relaxing power of clinical hypnosis to change one rhythm in the mind and one rhythm only. Remember my philosophy: change your thoughts and you can and you will change your destiny.

Let me explain it this way: in the mind you have two hemispheres, the left side and the right side. The mind works in a constant rhythm where thoughts – images – feelings – emotions volley so to speak back and forth from side to side. I can teach you how to change one rhythm and one rhythm only and you will start to lose the weight you desire: at first 1 ½ - 3 lbs per week and sometimes 3 – 4 pounds per week – slow: safe: effective!

The moment you begin to lose this weight right then and there you will start to feel better about yourself and you know exactly what that means. When you feel better about yourself it will help to stimulate your minds desire to want to do other positive things for yourself including exercise! You will once again start to experience more self-control, self-confidence and self-discipline. You

will make the important decision to also begin to live fully moment by moment and truly enjoy being alive each moment and no longer worried about things that happened in the past.

The past!!! Come-on now your past was then and that was a whole another time – decide that you life is starting now today and you make the decision to begin to live fully moment by moment and truly enjoy being alive each moment and no longer emotionally dependent on food. Yet enjoying the freedom and control of going anywhere you want eating anything you want whenever you want ½ only!

What does this mean? It means you now can go anywhere you want – eat anything you want ½ only! By eating ½ and leaving ½ you will drop your caloric intake by 50%. When you drop that amount of caloric intake your body weight has no choice but to modify down – true?

But, if you eat ½ and ½ only how on earth are you going to feel full? Remember it's in the mind not the stomach. During hypnosis I will be giving you suggestions that you mind now become completely satisfied by eating ½ and ½ only. Your appetite will relax down. Food will become less and less important to you. You will start eating more healthy and nutritious foods and therefore by reducing your caloric intake you body weight must and will go down. Oh, did I mention I also give suggestions for the stomach to relax smaller and to feel full faster: ½ way thru your meal – so if you continue choosing to overeat your stomach will feel tightness, tension, pressure and help you put the food down. Clever isn't it!

Your mind has all the power! All that you are is a direct result of the thoughts you have chosen to think for yourself. You hold the key to unlock that power to change your entire life's direction. Combined with the suggestions I give you, you will learn the hidden jewels of real success!

Consistency and repetition!!!

The time is now for you to decide and really decide based in truth to become and remain thin and slim again! Think about this: thin and slim again! That's right – again because you used to be and you were the one – the only one who made the choice to overeat and now its time to learn how to eat less, ½ only, feel totally content - in control and lose the weight you desire: slow, safe, effective!

The time is now for you to take the necessary action to realize the inner belief that your weight loss goal is definitely reachable. Your positive attitude combined with consistence & repetition will help keep you motivated - and guide you to the success you truly desire for yourself.

You can become thin and slim, you will become thin and slim because you want to become thin and slim *again* regardless of anything or anyone in your life. Therefore, nothing and no-one can ever influence the way you think and feel about yourself. This is your life - your choice – it's time for you to become the person you have always admired, the person you have always wanted to become, the real you that has been hidden inside long enough by excessive weight and finally at this

moment in time, you are ambitious, determined, and seriously motivated to set that person free!

Changing your thoughts will change your destiny... You have the power within your subconscious mind to change and control your own destiny from this day on. You can and you will change your life through the power of choice - power of thought!

THE POWER OF CHOICE

CREATE & MAINTAIN YOUR WEIGHT LOSS MOTIVATION

William Shakespeare - (*from* Hamlet 3/1)
To be, or not to be: that is the question:
Whether 'tis nobler in the mind to suffer
The slings and arrows of outrageous fortune,
Or to take arms against a sea of troubles

Are you ready to choose your kismet in life and leave behind the past? Are you willing to enact upon the goals that you are choosing for your self. You must set your mind into motion to achieve your true desires. This is where the power of hypnosis can help as well. It can teach you how to generate an abundance of positive energy and keep your mind on the takes you are choosing to achieve. It will help you to block out distractions and to remain concentrated and focused towards losing the weight you desire to lose for yourself.

No one can help you lose weight unless you choose to let them – with my seminar I always tell them it is vital that you choose to let the hypnosis work for you and in that choice you are actually learning how to hypnotize your own mind and

therefore control your own destiny and weight you want to lose!

If you choose to remain stagnant you can never lose the weight you want. You must motivate yourself thru the power of your own choices and the realization of you own weight loss goals.

Want to lose weight change the way you think around food. Don't want to lose the weight choose to stay the unhappy way you are!

When you see others who represent the physical image you would like to have you refer to them as lucky they can eat anything they want better metabolism... the truth is you are assuming that person has left their bodyweight up to chance ... you assume they have exerted no control over their own destiny...you assume their were no sacrifices. Make your first new choice right this minute: "I choose to no longer assume anything about anyone, including myself."

Becoming overweight did not happen to you by chance rather by direct choice of your own. You're the one who decided to overeat and choose the wrong foods and therefore you can change this direction at any given moment in time. It's your mind that got you into this and it's your mind that will get you out. At one point in your life you weighed exactly what you wanted to weigh, you were eating life was good-but then you consciously decided to start eating more and even as your body weight started to go up you said I'm not going to do this I'm going to control this now, yet you didn't, you continued to gain weight...how about when you realized your clothes were getting tighter –did

you just run out and buy new bigger sizes? And when you gain this weight do you feel attractive? NO! Then what you get depressed? What do you do when your depressed---eat! Then you get mad at yourself-what do you do when your angry—eat some more! Then it seems that you're starting over every Monday on some new diet. Intellectually you know that diets are temporary...in fact you go on a diet and you do lose weight but what happens when the diet ends? you end up going right back to your old eating thoughts...how about this do you eat when your depressed—sure but you also eat hen your happy...do you eat when all alone—sure but you also eat when your with others as well...in fact chances are you eat all the time... but does it matter when you eat or why you eat... absolutely not...it's the same problem its always been...quantity...simply put....eat too much your body weight goes up...eat less your body weight goes down...sounds simple right? But how do you eat less and feel content?

Let me ask you this: is fullness in your stomach? What about appetite and hunger? Absolutely not it's in your mind and you've always known that haven't you!

What if you could relax the way you think about food, make better healthier choices, and eat the foods you wanted yet still lost the weight you desired!!! Got your attention now don't I... finally a program where you can eat anything you like whenever you want and still lose the weight....is it when you eat? Why you eat? How you eat? Absolutely not...if you eat too much your body weight goes up...when you eat less your body weight goes down...my program think and

lose is specifically designed and time tested to enable you to lose weight simply by reducing your caloric intake and yet to feel satisfied where it truly counts—in the mind! Choose to set your mind in motion to become and remain thin and slim again!

As you learn the power of self-control and self-discipline with hypnosis you will be able to lose the weight that you desire. It will not matter where you are or what is going on in your personal life because that is going on anyway. There are no longer any cravings because you can in fact eat anything you want whenever you want! All negative emotions are gone...you see it, you want it, it's yours!

THE POWER OF THOUGHT

"Man is made or unmade by himself" James Allen

By making choices based in truth and which are positive in nature you can achieve beyond your wildest dreams! It is your choice and your choice alone that determines the direction of your life. This direction ultimately will determine your destiny!

It is imperative that you come to realize and understand that nothing happens by chance – rather by choice. Every situation in which you find yourself is the direct result of the choices you have made. The power to control your destiny lays within your own mind the power of your ability to think and to utilize the power of your thoughts.

When applying the power of thought control to weight loss you must first understand and accept the premise that you did not become overweight by chance rather by choice. It did not happen to you – you chose to overeat and to eat the wrong types of foods. Therefore, you can lose weight by making the choice to eat less and to choose foods that are good for you rather than foods that are rich and fattening.

If you were to use the premise of tracing your choices backward you will discover the truth that you are where you are at this point in your life by the decisions you have made. This begins to help you to understand the importance of the reason underneath the circumstances in your life today.

Depression, anger, low self-esteem, and being overweight are all the result of the negative application of thought control. According to James Allen if you plant the seeds of negativism you will most definitely grow weeds in your mind. Hence, if you choose to plant seeds of positive thought your mind will blossom into the person you truly want to be the real you inside that has been hidden long enough. If you choose do perceive no choice available to you the you arte choosing to accept the current conditions of your life and for that you can blame no one but yourself. On the other hand you can now choose to change the conditions of your life and move your mind towards a positive end for yourself and it is just as easy as making the choice to set your mind in motion to become happy, let go of anger, strengthen your self-esteem and begin to lose the weight that you desire.

Your emotions will always be found to be related directly to the inner state of your mind and the thoughts you choose to think. Understanding this premise is the most powerful awareness imaginable for it allows you to re-write – produce - & re-direct your entire destiny.

For example, when you are bothered and unhappy do not look into the environment around you look into your mind and analyze what choices you have made that are generating the feelings

you are having. e.g. angry, what are you thinking that is causing this anger? Depressed-what are you telling your mind inside that is making you fell depressed? Now change it...thought change will give you the power to refocus to feel happy by the thoughts you think...to be relaxed by the thoughts you think! Come-on its easier than you think. Try this: take a slow deep breath and when you exhale smile inside the mind as though you know something no-one else does...see how that makes you feel...your smiling...life is a little more tolerable...well think what you could do with the ultimate use of your mind!

When feeling overweight and unhappy look to the thoughts you are thinking and change them! When you are bothered and unhappy your mind simply cannot function properly. Time to change your thinking and plant those seeds of happiness and self-control & self-confidence & self-discipline turn your thoughts into blossoms of truth and happiness for self for no one else can or will! Good thoughts bear good fruit, bad thoughts bad fruit, says James Allen.

Look to the circumstances in your life to help you gain insight into why you are who you are. If you choose to improve the conditions of your life you must be willing to improve the way you think. Positive thoughts create positive results-negative thoughts create negative results. Depression and unhappiness is an indicator that you are out of harmony within your mind.

Being overweight is the effect of wrong thought in some direction. It is an indication that you are out of harmony with yourself. Your thoughts are

not as secret as you would like to believe for they quickly exhibit themselves in your physical appearance. No matter what your circumstances may be you can choose to change and reshape them. Your body is the servant of the min. Choose to overeat and your body will show the result.

Don't we all know individuals who are sick and depressed because they are so very negative about everything, everyone including them? They want sympathy because of all the unfortunate circumstances that have happened to them... they never realize they chose their condition and they can choose to change it but alas all too often they revel in their misery by choice and personal growth and development of happiness cease to be an option.

Positive thoughts that you now choose to think must become connected to energy to nurture it to fruition. Just thinking I will be happy when I lose 20 pounds and waiting for it to magically happen is of course ludicrous. Once making the choice to want to lose weight you then connect this positive thought to energy and motivate your mind to accomplish it. Motivation - ambition – determination to succeed for yourself and succeed you shall!

INSPIRATIONAL STORIES

www.Thinkandlose.com/testimonials

P.B. ...51 married, mother of three, grandmother of six, self-employed. "I come from a family of overweight women. I weighted 100 pounds when I was in kindergarten. Being overweight has been a part of my whole life. I've been on almost every diet known to man, including a stomach staple, which, like most diet pills worked backwards on me. I gained 50 pounds and almost died, only to have it unstapled two years later. The yoyo diets and the stapling and re-stapling caused other medical problems, and brought on my diabetes sooner. I ended up in the hospital with congestive heart failure. I knew then that I had to find another way to take control of my weight, and my life, when someone suggested I see the clinical hypnotist to the American Lung Association, Don Mannarino. Before Don's program my confidence level was nothing, I hated myself, I was a non-person. The main thing about being heavy and losing weight is that if you don't change you're the way you think you might as well forget it because its all coming back. After Don's program, Think and Lose I have lost 100 pounds and 79 inches. And now I'm me again I'm beautiful and some day I will be

gorgeous. Now I can play with my grandkids and you don't know what that is worth!

***L.A*....I had been overweight and my blood pressure was uncontrolled. I had to go to a sleep clinic and begin to use a C-Pap machine. At one time I weighted about 425 pounds if not more. A doctor discovered that my kidneys were only functioning at half their ability. My blood pressure, being uncontrolled for so long had damaged them. The doctors were talking about a possible kidney transplant if I didn't change my lifestyle. I was taking 39 pills (medication) a day because of all this. One of my doctors mentioned to me about Don Mannarino and the hypnosis program he was conducting for the American Lung Association. Not sure about hypnosis I went and immediately was put to ease by Don. I could feel his voice relaxing and calming me telling me that I can control my own destiny and that I can and I will lose the weight that I desired. I was amazed how good I felt and yet even more amazed that I was awake the whole time. The very next day I went to eat a hamburger and was totally shocked that I could barely eat half. I decided to wait a few weeks to weigh myself and to see if this was really working. I lost 38 pounds in the first month. Before starting Don's program I weighed 396 pounds and today I weigh about 260. I lost 140 pounds in eleven months on the Think and Lose weight loss program. I know that I can reach my goal of 220 pounds and that I will. I only take 4 pills a day now and there is no more talk about kidney transplant. My BP is under control and I feel so much better about myself. Without Don's program I may not have been alive to write this story. And all I did was reach over and hit a button**

to listen to Don's program and I had to go to bed anyway."

_R.G..._When I started Don's program I weighed in at 242 pounds. I felt terrible and I was tired all the time. Starting Dom's program things began to click right away for me and before you knew it I was on my way to losing weight. Three months after starting Think and Lose I had a physical at work and my cholesterol had gone down from 215 to 181 and my breathing efficiency went up from a dismal 79% to an incredible 99%. I also went from taking 1 ½ blood pressure pills per day down to ½ a pill. Within 8 months I managed to lose 62 pounds. My waist has gone down form a 42 overhang to a loose size 32-24. I am doing exercises and now I am up to 300 sit-ups and 150 pushups every other day. I am now the same weight that I was 40 years ago in high school. Everyone asks me how did I lose the weight and I tell them I listen to don's voice on the CD and everything seemed to fall right into place

_JP..._When it comes to weight loss I have tried different pills, different workouts, and a few diets. Only to keep losing the same 5-10 pounds over and over. I've come to a point where I research the weight loss method first only to find that more than likely it won't give you permanent results therefore I don't even give it a shot. Through my research I have learned that diet and exercise are the answer <u>not pills</u>. Easier said than done! Do to the fact the hypnosis stories were coming from two respectable women that I know I felt comfortable enough trying it myself. The hypnosis went well. I was impressed by how fast the process went. It was as if nothing had happened. Other than feeling

relaxed we didn't feel any different. In fact we even questioned whether or not the hypnosis worked. <u>As of December 2004 (5 months later) I have lost 24 pounds, 21 inches, and I have dropped 1-2 pant sizes.</u> This has been the easiest, fastest, and most enjoyable way to lose weight that I've tried. There were some struggles in the beginning, but for the most part it seems as if it was effortless and fun! I eat half of what I use to, haven't had to give up foods that I truly enjoy, I exercise at least 5 days a week (because I want to), and listen to the CD every night before bed. Oh, and my skeptic friends are proud of my success and have become believers. Let's not forget my husband, he enjoys the thinner me and says he can tell a difference in my self-confidence. Thank you Don Mannarino for offering a wonderful program.

***<u>JT...</u>*I weighed about 300 pounds. I am now happy to say with your help I have succeeded beyond my dreams...I now weigh 233 pounds that's a 67 pound weight loss thanks to your hypnotic skills! I would recommend this program to anyone who wants to lose weight easy and keep it off. I have been heavy all my life and your program is the most effective method I have found.**

***<u>JS...</u>*I am 61-years old and have been dieting for the past 45 years. As with so many overweight people, I have tried all the diets, bought all the books, taken amphetamines, joined several groups and they all worked for a while and then I'd return to my usual overweight self as soon as I stopped following the current food rules. Dieting can be a very dangerous for me because I went through a three-year period with bulimia where I'd binge and make myself vomit. I'm not proud**

of those years but must remember them as I am susceptible to problems controlling my food intake, understanding that there is no one magic number for my weight (my mind believes I should weight 128 pounds), and realizing that there are no good versus bad foods. Using the hypnosis has not caused me any stress in losing weight. This method could not only have changed my life but have saved my life. On April 7 I weighed 197 pounds and wore size 18 slacks. I did not expect to be here in December weighing 167 pounds and fitting into size 12 pants and even a couple pairs of size 10. Each time I would be weighed at the doctor, I was amazed that something this pain-free could be for real. I don't diet and I don't obsess about food anymore. I no longer have a list of so many foods that are forbidden. My attention was captured when while hypnotized Don told us our bodies were encased in cement -- no matter how hard I tried I couldn't move my legs or arms. When we got to the section about eating, the words half only - half only were repeated. The thought that there were no more forbidden foods and that I could eat what I wanted and when I wanted it, but half only seemed unbelievable to me. The day after the first hypnotism session, my daughter and her husband took me to Niagara Falls. In the restaurant I said would anyone like to split a meal with me? Those words had never come out of my mouth before and I know they had never been in my brain before. They just came out. It just felt natural asking that question. Since the hypnosis sessions when I go to a restaurant, I ask for a box for my food and put half in the box before I start eating. This gives me another meal for another time. Today I weigh myself only when at the doctor's offices or to the recreation center

because I still have problems with the perfect numbers where weight comes in. Each time I have been weighed I have weighed less than the time before. Today I weigh 165 pounds, 32 pounds less than the first night of hypnotism. After a life of dieting, binging, purging and feeling bad about my body, this new way of thinking constantly amazes me. After all the tricks I tried to play with food to find the perfect solution, it seems very strange that I never heard about eating what I wanted but eating half only. Certainly seems like a logical thing to do. With the hypnotism I find it possible to do almost all the time.

JW...**As of today November 2, I have lost 12 ½ pounds. My goal is 9 ½ more pounds, and at the rate I am going I'm not concerned about achieving this goal. (UPDATE: Lost 22 lbs by mid December and met her goal) My mother is in a nursing home and when I was at a craft/bake sale there a few weeks ago the activities director was pushing chocolate covered raisins (one of my all time favorites). I told her I couldn't have chocolate because it didn't agree with me. With a sympathetic look she asked, did it make me real sick, and I said no, it makes me real fat. We both got a chuckle out of that statement. I really wasn't interested in those raisins, although I felt I would be in control if I did want a couple. Since you have instilled in us that we can eat whatever we want only half I don't feel deprived. This is what is so special about this program. We don't take Magic Pills (as I saw advertised on the internet today) and we can eat anything we want, only half. I also feel that I am eating better foods now. If I am hungry I try to find something healthy to satisfy my hunger. I actually find that there aren't as many times now**

during the day when I am really hungry. The nice part is I doubt if anyone has noticed a change in my eating habits, because I'm not moaning and groaning about this awful diet I am on and I am eating just like everyone else. Well, maybe not quite like everyone else, but I am eating the same foods, just only a lot less. I was just telling my husband this morning I don't know why everyone that needs to lose weight doesn't try this approach. He said he gave me credit for doing it and I told him, it certainly hasn't been hard. I don't even use the word "diet" when I talk about what I am doing. To me it is just a great way of life.

RG... **I started to lose weight immediately. Over the next 12 months I lost a total of 70 pounds! I am so very happy I feel just great and I owe it all to you. I would strongly recommend you and your hypnosis program for weight loss to everyone.**

TB...**I've lost 36 lbs., on my scale! I lost the weight in 3 months! I think the program works because of its simplicity. I have only changed one thing since the first time I was hypnotized. Now I am able to eat *HALF ONLY*. I can still eat the same foods I have always had if I want to and when I eat out I order whatever I want, including desert if I want. It is fantastic! I have recommended this to others and when ever I hear people talking about trying to lose weight I can't wait to tell them about your program and how it has worked for me. I tell people about it because I have found it to be an easy and effective way to lose weight.**

WR...**After many years of trying to find a weight loss program that was right for me, I finally found**

the weight loss program conducted by hypnotist Don Mannarino for weight loss through hypnosis. Don's program made losing weight painless and simple. I simply ate whatever I wanted, whenever I wanted, but only half as much! The pounds literally started coming off each week. After a year, I lost 60 pounds and I feel great! Also, I found myself making healthier choices when eating. I would highly recommend this program to anyone who has tried other programs and failed. It made losing weight so easy. Thanks again Don!

GETTING STARTED

Decide right now to let go of the past and everything and everyone with it...that your life begins now today and you now finally decide to begin to live fully moment by moment and truly enjoy being alive each moment. Decide now to change directions in your life to start once again to control your thoughts and your actions. Know that nothing happens by chance only by choice your choice! Decide to no longer be a victim of your circumstances rather decide now to start to control them. Decide to control your destiny.

Think of an exact number you truly would like to weigh again. That number sets into motion your subconscious mind. The number represents an image and that image is the real you...the real you that has been hidden inside...and now finally you are deciding to set free.

Repeat daily this affirmation: I can become thin, I will become thin, I am going to become thin, because I want to be thin.

Use the simple principle for positive change: I can, I will, I am...because I want. The time is now

for you to release the positive force inside your mind to finally get what you want from life.

Motivation to succeed is like a passion inside you fan that passion and you can and you will achieve any goal you choose to achieve. Be honest with your self. Start to recognize and develop and strengthen your positive motivation to succeed at what it is that you are using now to decide to accomplish though the power of your own mind...the power of your own thoughts. What you put into your mind always becomes true. Its time to decide to let go of old negative thoughts that are self-defeating and set your mind towards the development of positive self-development!

It is time to seek out and discover your true mind's potential and develop it. Surround yourself with positive influences at every opportunity. Time to become the person you have always wanted to become the happy you!

You and you alone are now the writer, director and producer of your own destiny! Have courage in your decision and determination to succeed and succeed you shall! What you put into your mind with feeling and determination always becomes true-follow your instincts to succeed. Time to create the conditions of your life no longer to just be a passive victim of them!!!

Become thin and slim again- you used to be you changed it and now its time for you to change to back!

This chapter contains the overview of my think and lose seminar for weight loss.

The very first thing I recommend is that if you are on a diet for medical or psychological reasons prescribed by your physician than that diet must take medical priority.That aside no more dieting. Certainly by now you are a professional when it comes to dieting. You go on a diet and you lose weight, the problem however occurs when the diet ends for you end up going right back to your old eating habits. It doesn't mater when you eat or why you eat or how you eat – it's the quantity. I tell everyone to simply this it's your mind that got you into this it's the mind that can & will get you out of it. People have a tendency to eat when depressed but they also eat when they are happy! People eat when alone but also when they are with others! In fact most individuals who are overweight have the tendency to eat all the time regardless of what's going on in there personal lives. Think about this: when you eat too much your body weight goes up right – and when you eat less your body weight goes down. So why is it that something so simple becomes so complicated for you. Why is it when you're around food you eat too fast & you overeat! How do you feel when you overeat? Do you get depressed? What do you do when depressed eat? Then you get mad at yourself and then you eat again. Then you probably say this diet doesn't work I'll go on another one next Monday! Chances are its only Monday afternoon and you had stayed up late on Sunday night to eat everything you could get your hands on before starting the 'new' diet. Ever go on a diet on Tuesday at 12 noon... don't think so! Diets are OUT! From now on you will have the self-control & the self-confidence to go anywhere you want, eat anything you want & whenever you want. No guilt no anxiety no stress...

you see it you want it- its yours. I need to get into your subconscious mind and change one rhythm.

The mind contains two hemispheres: the right side & the left side. The brain works in a natural rhythm back and forth side to side. Through the power of hypnosis combined with your motivation I can change the rhythm. For example: instead of your current rhythm eating all or none I can change the rhythm to eating half & leaving half. Think about this, eating ½ and leaving ½ half only! Right there you will reduce your caloric intake by 50%. When you reduce the caloric intake by 50% your body weight has no choice but to modify down. Its always been about calories. 3500 calories is a pound of body fat. Eat to much body weight goes up right – so eat less...no denial no restriction!

So now your thinking this is great I can go anywhere I want eat anything I ant whenever I want and still lose weight – by eating ½ only! But, how will I feel full with only ½? What about my stomach appetite? Hunger? Fullness? Simple: appetite-hunger-fullness is not in the stomach it is in the mind! I know where it is and the rhythm to change it and your going to let me right? Your motivation and level of internal honesty and truth to want to lose weight will bring you the success you desire.

For many of you it will be a great deal easier to put ½ on the plate and eat it all. So often you just like to see the plate empty. When eating out and you feel full ½ way thru your meal do not worry about wasting the food. If you eat it you will only continue to 'waist' it around your waist! Make sense?

I know what many of you are thinking,'how can I waist food there are kids starving in the world' we have all heard this from parents, & teachers, however the fact is this: If you choose to overeat because you do not want to waist food & have kids starving, and you end up eating it all where does that leave the starving children then? Come on think, you end up gaining the weight because you ate all the food and the kids end up really starving because there was none left for them. It doesn't work! It never did and it never will.

Be realistic have your cake and eat it too! ½ only...in no time your stomach will actually begin to shrink smaller and you will feel the sensation of fullness easier but real fullness is in the mind and I will give you suggestions to help you think full by eating less.

There are thousands of people just like you. They use my program to put ½ on the plate and eat it all. They derive extraordinary happiness from having true control over the quantity of the foods they choose to eat. Nothing happens by chance becoming overweight was a direct choice – well so is becoming thin and slim again.

That's right thin & slim AGAIN! You used to be, and you were the one, the only one who chose to eat too much and gained the weight. Becoming overweight did not happen to you by chance rather by direct choice your choice! You got yourself into this and now you forgot how to get your self out of it.

If you let me, I can teach you the true ancient art of mind control – hypnosis! When done right hypnosis is the most relaxing feeling you could ever imagine. Way more soothing than most people realize. During hypnosis your subconscious mind becomes susceptible to suggestions. With regards to the suggestions to become thin and slim again suggestions you truly want to hear your mind then become hyper-susceptible and that makes it exceptionally easy for you to reach success.

Remember this: it's your mind that got you into this and its your mind that will get you out! You did not gain weight b chance rather by choice and now its time to make the decision to choose to eat less and lose the weight you desire. At the same time you will learn how to end your craving for sugars, sweets, candy pastry pop and salty snacks. Learn how to begin choosing foods that are good for you rather than foods that are rich and fattening.

As you learn the art of thought control with my think and lose weight loss program you will come to learn how to think of an exact number you truly want to weigh – rather than think in terms of pounds to lose or dress sizes or belt loops. The number you choose to weigh will give your mind direction it also represents the image of your desire to become thin and slim again. You used to be you changed it once and now its time to change it backwards as only you can.

Through my over 30 years of experience as a clinical hypnotist to some of the biggest health organizations in the world, The AHA 1978-1986 & the ALA 1986 - 2005 I have had the unique

opportunity to help thousands of individuals reach their goals. I know and I have always known that I can hypnotize anybody, anyplace anywhere! Learning the conditioned response of relaxing hypnosis is actually the easy part – what truly determines your success is to thy own self be true! You and you alone know the real truth inside – do you or do you not want to lose weight? Are you ready to lose weight regardless of what's going on in your personal & professional life?

Isn't it time to let go of the past and everything and everyone with it? Your past was then and that was a whole another time. Your life begins now today and its time to make the all important decision to begin to live fully moment by moment and truly appreciate being alive each moment. The time is now to learn in a positive way how to strengthen and develop your level of self-confidence, self-control & self-discipline.

If your answer to any of the following questions is yes then the Think & Lose program is definitely for you!

Do you want to learn how to eat less and choose foods that are good for you rather than foods that are rich and fattening? Do you want to learn the difference between real hunger & psychological hunger before you eat instead of after? Do you want to end late night snacking? Do you want to end cravings for salty, sweet junk foods? Do you want to end self-sabotage behavior? Do you want to end emotional eating? Do you want to end psychological dependence of food?

The program Think and Lose contains a great deal more weight loss information in terms of specificity regarding the learning of new eating thoughts & behaviors and the relaxing technique of clinical hypnosis. For your convenience visit:

www.Thinkandlose.com

WHERE YOU GO FROM HERE

VISIT DON MANNARINO'S THINK & LOSE HYPNOSIS WEB SITE:

www.Thinkandlose.com

BIBLIOGRAPHY

SUGGESTED READING

The Surgeon General's Call to Action to Prevent & Decrease Overweight and Obesity, U.S. Department of Health & Human Services (2001)
http://www.surgeongeneral.gov/topics/obesity/

The Power of Choice: Helping To Make Healthy Eating and Fitness Decisions, U.S. Food and Drug Administration and U.S. Department of Agriculture's Food and Nutrition Service (2003)
http://www.fns.usda.gov/tn/resources/power of choice.html

Obesity Research Statistics For The United States
ASD & CDC Research Statistics On Obesity In The United States. In 1962, research statistics showed that the percentage of obesity in America's population.
www.americansportsdata.com/obesityresearch.asp

The American Heart Association and the Robert Wood Johnson Foundation this sourcebook, *A Nation at Risk: Obesity in the United States.*

American Heart Association National Center
File Format: PDF/Adobe Acrobat - View as HTML
(NHANES [2003-2004], NCHS; JAMA. 2006;295:1549-

1555.) •. On the basis of data from NHANES, NCHS
www.americanheart.org/downloadable/heart/1197994908531FS16OVR08.pdf

WHO. Obesity and Overweight. Fact Sheet No. 311. www.who.int/mediacentre/factsheets/fs311/en/print.html)

Obesity in Adulthood and Its Consequences for Life Expectancy:
Drs. Peeters, Barendregt, Mackenbach, and Bonneux:
Analysis/and/interpretation/of/the/data:
www.annals.org/cgi/content/abstract/138/1/24

APA Division 30 - Society of Psychological Hypnosis
Homepage of the American Psychological Associations Division 30, Psychological Hypnosis. The site provides a description of the division/
www.apa.org/about/division/div30.html - 17k

AMA: American Medical Association (1958). 'Council on Mental Health: Medical use of Hypnosis', JAMA, Sep 13,1958: 186-189.

JAMA, the Journal of the American Medical Association
Ahighly cited weekly medical journal that publishes peer-reviewed original medical research.
jama.ama-assn.org/

The Medical Recognition of Hypnotherapy
In 1892, the British Medical Association (BMA) responded to growing ... a more extensive statement on the medical uses of hypnosis/
www.ukhypnosis.com/Medical-Status.htm - 16k

Special Report on Hypnotherapy
File Format: PDF/Adobe Acrobat - View as HTML
The Medical & Scientific Status of Hypnotherapy. (Copyright © Donald Robertson 2000-2005) ... the medical establishment's views on hypnotherapy.

www.ukhypnosis.com/Events/Special%20Report%20on%20Hypnotherapy.pdf

Obesity and Overweight: Introduction | DNPAO | CDC
Overweight and Obesity, Trends, Contributing Factors, Health Consequences, Economic Consequences, State-Based Programs, Recommendations.
www.cdc.gov/nccdphp/dnpa/obesity/
US FDA/CFSAN - Calories Count and Keystone Report
Documents and Resources on FDA's Obesity Working Report,
www.cfsan.fda.gov/~dms/nutrcal.html

Conscious - What Is the Conscious Mind
In Freud's psychoanalytic theory of personality, the conscious mind includes everything that inside of our awareness...
psychology.about.com/od/cindex/g/def_conscious.htm

Psychoanalytic Theory - The Conscious and Unconscious Mind
According to psychoanalysis, thoughts and motivations outside of our awareness influence our behavior. Learn more about Freud's-theory-of-the-conscious-and-subconscious-mind.
psychology.about.com/od/theoriesofpersonality/a/consciousuncon.htm

Conscious mind - definition of Conscious mind in the Medical
Online English dictionary. What is Conscious mind? Meaning of Conscious/mind/medical/term.
medical-dictionary.thefreedictionary.com/Conscious+mind

Sleep Disorders Information & Resources
Sleep disorder community providing information and resources on-sleep-disorders.
www.talkaboutsleep.com/sleep-disorders/

The History of Hypnosis
This is an overview of hypnosis history and when it was first used in the healing professions and how the techniques changed over the years.
www.essortment.com/all/hypnosishistory_rcdg.htm

Complete Timeline/History of Hypnosis
http://news.google.com/archivesearch?hl=en&rlz=1G1GGLQ_ENUS271&ie=UTF8&q=of+hypnosis&um=1&scoring=t&sa=X&oi=archive&ct=title

The Origin and History of Hypnosis
The scientific history of hypnosis began about 1775 with Anton Mesmer, whose name is still attached to it.
ezinearticles.com/?The-Origin-and-History-of-Hypnosis&id

HYPNOSIS
T X Barber, "Hypnosis: A Scientific Approach" (Van Nostrand Reinhold 1969). T X Barber, Nicholas P Spanos, and John F Chaves, "Hypnotism: Imagination...
www.hutch.demon.co.uk/hypnosum.htm

Theodore Xenophon Barber | American Journal of Clinical Hypnosis
Theodore Xenophon Barber from American Journal of Clinical Hypnosis in Health provided free by Find Articles.
findarticles.com/p/articles/mi_qa4087/is_200604/ai_n17188647

Theodore X. Barber (1927–2005)
Theodore Xenophon Barber, one of the most prolific and influ-ential researchers in the field of hypnosis, died unexpectedly on
content.apa.org/journals/amp/61/2/175.pdf

You Are Getting Sleepy: Dr. Theodore X. Barber 1927-

2005
from the NY Times: Dr. Barber developed what became career-long studies of hypnosis in the 1960's, while conducting research at the Medfield Foundation.
hypnospin.blogspot.com/2005/09/dr-theodore-x-barber-1927-2005.html

Shakespeare - To be, or not to be: that is the question
William Shakespeare - To be, or not to be (from Hamlet 3/1). To be/or-not-to/be-that/is-the/question...
www.artofeurope.com/shakespeare/sha8.ht

Official Bela Lugosi Website - Home
Welcome to the Officialy Licensed Bela Lugosi Website, everything you want to know about the famous actor.
www.lugosi.com/lugosihomepage.html

Richest Man In Babylon Book by George Clason
Customer Reviews of "Richest Man In Babylon" by George S Clason - Submit your review online. No Reviews - Book Review
www.woopidoo.com/reviews/books/george-clason/index.htm

James Allen Home Page
Biography of James Allen (1864-1912), author of As a Man Thinketh and many other books. Site has several books by him that can be read online.
jamesallen.wwwhubs.com/

10568194R00055

Printed in Great Britain
by Amazon